MIDWEST FRONTIER STORIES

- Collection 2

A treasury of first hand stories in original wording by the frontier settlers of the Midwest about the period of 1815-1845.
 (Primarily South East Iowa and North East Missouri)

- FIRST EDITION -

Compiled and edited by
Ed Scharff and
Leila Scharff

b

Midwest Frontier Stories – Collection 2
Copyright © 2018 by Ed and Leila Scharff

ISBN-13   **9780999494516**
ISBN-10   **0999494511**
Library of Congress Control Number: 2017916914

Website: www.midwestfrontierstories.com

Manufactured in the United States of America

c

d

Dedication

Midwest Frontier Stories - Collection 2
Is dedicated to General Lawrence Sullivan Ross.
      Son of Shapley Prince Ross
      Grandson to Shapley Ross-
            who founded of Moscow Mills, MO
      Nephew of Giles Oldham Sullivan

1838	Born in Bentonsport, Iowa - Sept 27
1839	Moved to Texas, Milam County
1849	Settled at Waco, Texas
1856	Attended Baylor University
1859	Graduated from Wesleyan University, Alabama
1860	Captain in Mounted Texas Rangers
1860	Recovered Cynthia Ann Parker from Comanches
1861	Enlisted in Company G, Sixth TX Calvary
1863	Promoted to Confederate Brigadier General
1873-1875	Sheriff of McLennan County, TX
1876	Member of the Texas Constitutional Convention
1880-1882	Texas state Senator
1886-1890	19th Governor of Texas
1891-1898	President of Texas A&M
1898	Died in College Station, Texas A&M on Jan 3

Special gratitude to
- Missouri and Iowa State archives
- Iowa Libraries: Keokuk, Burlington, Montrose, Dubuque and Fort Madison
- Missouri Libraries: Kahoka, Palmyra, St Louis County and St. Charles.
- Roger McPherson and Mike Miller for sharing the ledger of Sweet Home.
- Public domain images from various sources

Preface

Learn history direct from those who LIVED IT!

Like in Collection 1, this is a collection of stories written by the pioneer frontiersmen of the Wisconsin Territory, southeast Iowa and northeast Missouri. All stories are un-altered from their original wording, so that you can have the fun of finding your own GEMS of knowledge and NUGGETS of truth hidden in them.

When reading, remember to place yourself at the time of original publication and think of the time these stories were written about. Most settlements, fur buyers and Trading Posts were along rivers and streams. Virtually nothing of today existed in the Midwest, no roads or bridges, no stores, only the fist, knife and muzzleloading flintlock existed for protection. Community was required to survive, Law was community based, and the Frontiersmen had to find a way to survive with their limited resources!

These stories can give a good understanding of the life on the Midwest Frontier. Some may be exaggerated, but they may well be truer than "twisted" history written by those who could benefit.

Many stories contain genealogical data that is almost never found, such as hair and eye color, body build, distinguishing features, character, birth location and movement upon the frontier.

We hope you enjoy learning about the Old (mid)WEST as much as we have.

Sincerely,

Ed and Leila Scharff

Table of Contents

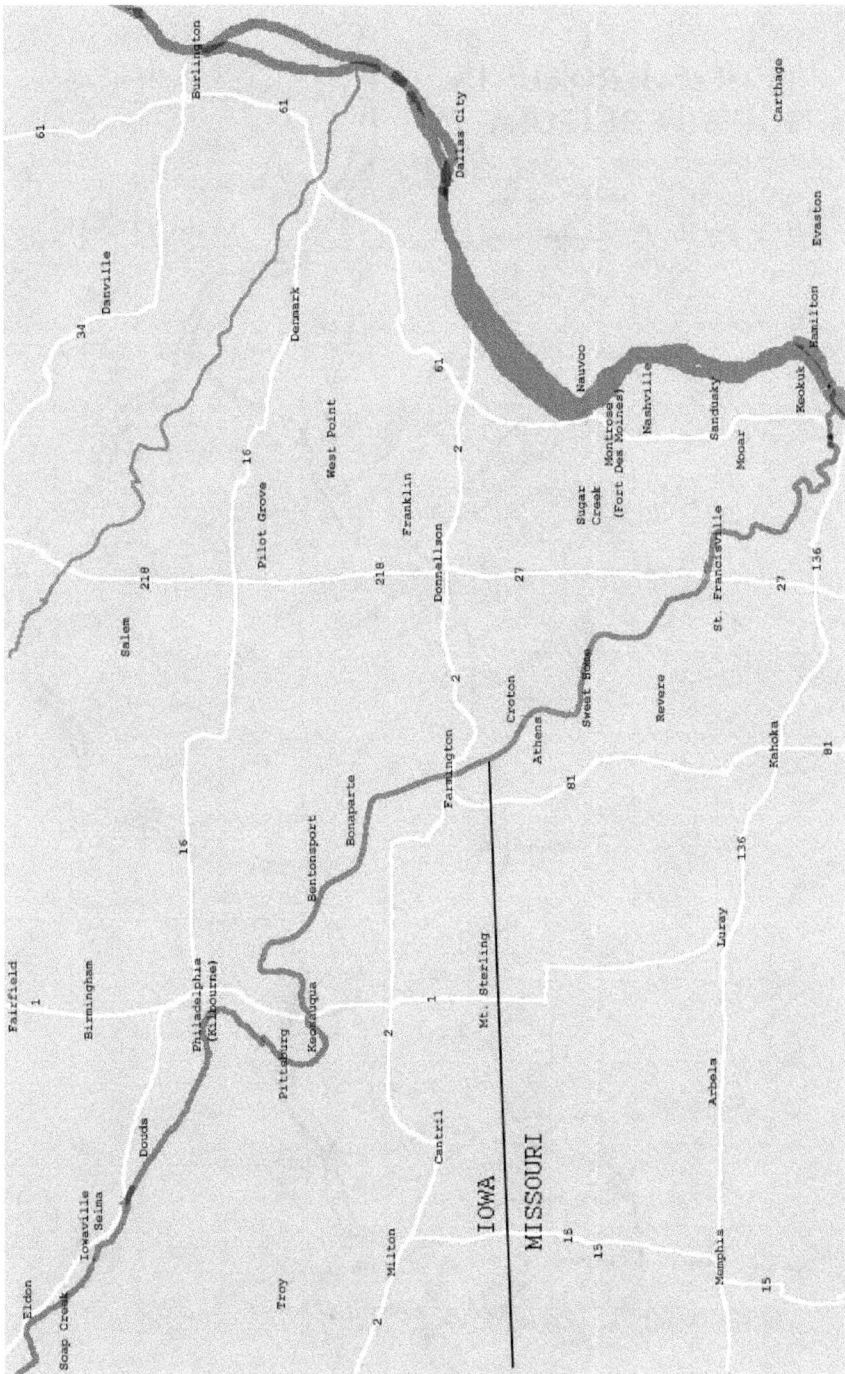

k

FEDERAL ROADS IN
IOWA TERRITORY
1839

Agency Road — — — —
Military Road ————

Prairie du Chien

Scale
0   10

WISCONSIN

Cedar River

Maquoketa River

Buffalo Creek

North River

Dubuque

Cascade

Monticello

Martelle

Wapsapinicon River

Anamosa

Iowa River

Solon

Mt. Vernon

Iowa City

English River

Cedar River

MISSISSIPPI RIVER

Bloomington
(Muscatine)

Long Creek

Skunk River

Crawfordsville

ILLINOIS

Crooked Creek

Little Cedar Creek

Agency
City

Iowaville

Mt. Pleasant

Washington

Burlington

Keosauqua

Ft. Madison

Des Moines River

Camp Des Moines

MISSOURI   St Francisville

1

Peter Pierre's Great Race

In the JAN. 7, 1870 edition of THE GATE CITY, A.W. Harlan
tells of Indian dress and of the six mile run of Peter and other
super-human feats that he has witnessed.

The following little incident, that I shall try to relate,
occurred in January, 1836, just where the little village of
Philadelphia now stands in Van Buren County, Iowa:

At the time of which I am writing there was three Indian
trading houses at that point. Shropshire, of Palmyra,
Missouri, was represented by James Jordan and Hiram
Taylor, and just then there was only Daniel McMullen to
represent Phelpes. The American Fur Company were
represented by a Mr. Wells. Their house was on the
opposite side of the river and rather below.

I had went up there just to be going, and as the weather
was cold, stayed several days. The next day after my
arrival the Indians come down from somewhere near White
Breast Falls, where they had a temporary encampment
while out hunting.

Some ten or a dozen Sac and Fox Indians had found and
killed two Sioux Indians. This ended their hunt. They came
pouring down into the main camp - some from fear of the
Sioux, and others perhaps, to enjoy being lionized[1] and
wear laurels[2]. The laurels they wore did not correspond
with my previous conceived opinion.

---

[1] give a lot of public attention and approval to (someone); treat as a celebrity
[2] wreath or crown and worn on the head as an emblem of victory or mark of
honor in classical times

1

The laurels they wore consisted of lind[3] shavings, made by taking a piece of Basswood, and, with a sharp knife drawn up, the shaving would curl. Then another and so on successively until it formed a bunch as large as a man's two fists, with one end of the block remaining solid. It was fastened to each side of the head. This rendered them conspicuous among their fellow savages. And such a stiff[4] as a young brave can put on, on such occasions may be imagined, and then the Indian that may have taken the scalp[5] is, by law, allowed to wear an additional skunk tail on his leggings[6] when dressed up for important occasions. That is one skunk tail for every scalp he may have taken.

One thing more I noticed, that the Indians that had big bunches of shavings on their heads were remarkably popular with the (Shushkese) young women.

For some three or four days they had feasted and frolicking[7]. Then came an alarm, though a false alarm. The Sioux were coming and such running and yelling I have never witnessed before. Here I learned that they were cowardly as well as vain.

Peter Pierre was a large stout young man, that had no more business at the trading houses than myself, but he happened to get scared a little worse and started from Jordan's house to run angling down the river. The river was

---

[3] wood from a linden or basswood tree
[4] Slang- racehorse or someone sure to lose.
[5] the skin covering the head (hair), excluding the face.
[6] buckskin leg coverings
[7] play and move about cheerfully, excitedly, or energetically

partly open. He did not turn for water. Across to Wells' house they saw him coming and closed the doors. He ran once round the house and then struck a beeline in the Southwest direction. There was snow on the ground. He went through the brush and over broken ground scarcely deviating from a straight line. He started about ten o'clock, and by three he had run to some place on Fox River, not far from where Milton is now situated and stopped at a solitary Indian Lodge[8] overnight, or he must have frozen.

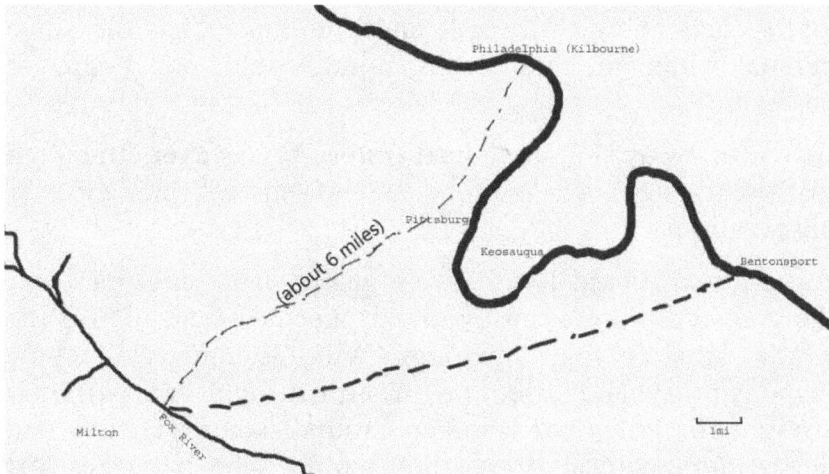

The next day the Indian brought him over to Giles Sullivan's cabin where Bentonsport is at present. How differently a report or an alarm will operate on different individuals. When the alarm first came old Daniel McMullen did not scare worth a cent. He caught his rifle, examined the priming then caught up and commenced loading another gun and asked me to step out and see if the Sioux were in sight. I looked first for the Sioux - there were none in sight. Then I looked at the retreating Indians. There were many on the river running but Peter Pierre led the van and as he broke through the thin ice on the riffle[9], his heels threw large pieces higher than his head.

---

[8] the house of the Midwest Indian's made of sticks and bark.

[9] a rocky or shallow part of a stream or river with rough water.

Now, if any person should ever read this sketch, I should not blame them if they accuse me of exaggeration or positive falsehood. But, gentle reader, just hold in while I try to argue the case.

Have you ever seen a person, prostrated[10] with fever, whilst the fever was raging, exhibit extraordinary strength, and when the fever has abated[11], be almost perfectly helpless? And, again, have you ever observed that a crazy person, while on their worst spells will perform acts of agility and exhibit strength and endurance that the same person when in their right mind could not begin to perform.

I am not aware that a medical fraternity has ever attempted to investigate such matters, but if so, let me add my observations.

A man well scared loses his judgment, if he ever had any, the connection between mind and muscle is cut off for the whole time being, his legs will assume the whole responsibility and direction of affairs, and run perfectly straight for miles over broken ground, where, if they had begun their natural mind, they would soon have got lost and wandered around.

One thing more I have observed: After a fellow has been doing tall running, he invariably has an extraordinary appetite for several days. This seems to be necessary to recuperate the waste of muscular power expended in running.

As for myself I do not remember of ever having performed but one extraordinary feat. About 1855 I was over in Missouri with my oldest boy, gathering some cedar bushes on the bluff. I had cautioned the boy to keep a sharp lookout for snakes.

We were both busy pulling up cedar bushes; I had just started for a small one, with my right foot on a ledge perhaps one foot

---

[10] reduced (someone) to extreme physical weakness
[11] Reduced to normal

4

high, with my left foot already raised, just going to step down, my eye caught sight of a large yellow rattlesnake ready coiled

for a stroke[12]; only one second more and my left foot would have been on a large snake with nine rattles. Instead of stepping on that snake I lit on the ground more than 10 feet from the snake though a little downhill. The snake was soon killed. My boy saw me make that extra ordinary jump and complimented me accordingly; we measured the distance. I could not come anywhere near performing that feat again. In short I am of the opinion that those extraordinary feats are only performed when there is but little if any connection between the mind and muscle, although I am aware that most men take to reverse view of the case, and I shall now leave it before the regular debating Society.

---

[12] Strike or attempt to bite

John Jasper "Red John" Collard

*In THE DAILY GATE CITY on Feb 11 1872, A.W. Harlan tells
a story about John Collard, who was becoming a pest in the
community and how they convinced him to leave.*

John Collard was one of the early pioneers of the Des
Moines Valley. I cannot say that he was a settler, because
be never settled long in one place, indeed, I do not
remember that he ever had a claim. He was raised about St.
Charles, Pike and Lincoln counties, Missouri. He came
here in the spring of 1835. At that time he was about
nineteen years of age. He was just six feet as he stood flat-
footed and erect. His head hung a little back of the
perpendicular, covered with a mass of very red hair, a
freckled face, high cheek bones, deep blue eyes and rather
large thick lips, which did not quite cover a splendid set of
ivory[13]. He weighed from two hundred to two hundred and
twenty pounds. The difference in weight was owing[14]
principally to the amount of eatables[15] that he may have
come in contact with in the twenty-four hours previous to
being weighed, for I never heard of him complaining of
being unwell. He had a fair share of mother wit, was a
pretty close observer of things in general, but without
education, being barely able to spell in three syllables; was
fond of argument and in debating made a good many cute
observations. In short, it was afterwards said that John
Collard was no slouch. He was decidedly a happy man. He
never borrowed trouble about tomorrow. He let every day
provide for itself; with him "it was come day, go day: God
and Sunday." I remember once of inquiring of him where
he was boarding at that time. His only reply was a comical
grin. I then asked him where he was staying. After a time

---

[13] Slang for teeth
[14] Due to, or was caused by
[15] Slang for Food

7

he replied, "Oh around one place and another. Where the pot biles[16] the strongest, there I stay the longest," He was a good judge of a horse, and went to every horse race that he could hear of within a radius of twenty miles. He generally bet his pile and nearly always won, but then his piles were small, seldom exceeding five dollars. He was not guilty of any particular extravagance in his dress, which visually consisted of a coarse shirt, a pair of pants made from ordinary bed ticking and a linsey wammus[17] or hunting shirt. He seldom wore a hat, his wonderful crop of red hair rendering that a superfluous[18] article. With moccasins on his feet and plenty to eat, he defied both wind and weather, and with a single blanket he could sleep on a punchon[19], floor the coldest nights and was never known to shiver.

He was fond of whisky[20], generally drank all that was given to him, but his friends never gave him enough to make him drunk; at least, I never heard of him being drunk. He was a good hand at horse raising, was considered equal to two common men, always went when invited and often, when he was not invited. When meal time came, he could not be persuaded to sit down until he was satisfied it was the last table. Then he was never known to leave while anything in the shape of eatables remained upon the table. I hope the foregoing description will sufficiently illustrate his characteristics. And thus he had lead[21] a happy life for some eighteen or twenty months. But perfect happiness on this earth has seldom

---

[16] He means BOILS.
[17] Warm linen work jacket resembling a Cardigan
[18] unnecessary, especially through being more than enough.
[19] Split log or roughly formed lumber
[20] Irish spelling of Scottish Whisky, also the spelling for American whiskey.
[21] To be in charge or command of "his life"

been of long continuance, and his day of tribulation[22] came at last.

The winter of 1836-7 was the time, and about where Iowaville now stands, was the place of tribulations, and I might add his exploits, that may render his name immortal.

Now, in order that the reader may fully comprehend the situation, I must introduce the names of several persons, too well known in the Des Moines valley to require an introduction in any crowd at that time or even now; James Jordan, Peter Avery, Wm. Avery, T. Jefferson Jordan, Wm. Phelps, a Mr. McPherson, Henry Netherton, and several others. It is enough to say of them that they were there, and whatever duties may have been assigned to any one of them it was faithfully performed.

As Jeff Jordan was prime mover and presiding genius on this occasion, a few words of him may be necessary. He was a Kentuckian by birth, said to be a good Latin scholar and a tolerably well-read historian, and when studying devilment or telling a tall yarn, looked very sober, but when concocting[23] a wicked hoax he looked truly sanctified.

These men just named were Indian traders[24], located at that place. The season of active trade was over: the Indians had all returned from their fall hunt, and disposed of their furs and peltries, and the time for a general relaxation with the Indians as well as traders had come.

A good deal of card playing had been done, and whisky had been drank, mixed up with some horse racing. This called John Collard to that point.

---

[22] a state of great trouble or suffering.

[23] Create or devise

[24] someone who trades goods with the Indians, usually for a fur company.

John had acquired some knowledge of the Indian language. He had examined all their tackies[25], as he called their horses, as well as the horses of the Traders, and when a race was won, John nearly always won some money, and seemed fonder of winning money from the Traders than of the Indians. Then he was just smart enough not to give them a chance to win it back at playing cards.

Now, such men as Bill Phelps, Pete Avery, Jim Jordan and others could not be expected to endure this state of affairs a great while. Those Traders were as liberal a set of fellows, in many respects, as the world ever produced. Though their provisions had been boated many weary miles, and sometimes carried on packhorses, they were always free with comers and goers. There were two trading houses and one whisky shop, and John Collard would go and billet[26] himself on one house and stay until the grub would become scarce; then go to another house and give them the privilege of entertaining him a while, and so on, in succession, and then win their money at nearly every horse race. This state of affairs set them to thinking, and they may have done some talking. But Jeff Jordan and John Collard soon became fast friends, to all appearance. Jeff Jordan backed John Collard in everything; in short, he seemed willing to go his bottom dollar on John against the world.

At the time of which I am writing John Tollman, who had a half-breed wife, lived on a knoll about a mile Northeast of Iowaville. Old Van Caldwell, the father of H. Clay Caldwell, was living about a mile above Iowaville, on the bank of the river, and old Keokuk, one of the principal chiefs of the Sauk and Fox Nations of Indians had his principal Village on the upland, a little back of

---

[25] Marsh Tacky- rare breed of South Carolina horse descended from Spanish colonial horses

[26] a place, usually a civilian's house or other nonmilitary facility, where soldiers are lodged temporarily.

Independent[27]. He was about 40 years of age; was a polygamist[28] - that is, he had at the time five wives, three of them large, fat squaws, near his own age, and one about ten years younger, also large and corpulent[29]. Then he had one wife perhaps some seventeen or eighteen years of age, and rather pretty. He called her his tit-bit[30].

It may be as well here to admit that there were reports circulated among the Traders but some of those Indian women were not as virtuous as Caesar's wife is said to have been, and some of the Traders boasted of their adventures in such a way as to excite Collard's curiosity; and then, to have a correct idea of the whole situation, you must bear in mind that in some respects John Collard was remarkably developed.

The weather was moderate, and almost a continual string of Indian squaws, young and old, were passing from the village to the trading house. One day Jeff Jordan made an important discovery. He had just found out what the Collard was made for. All hands were anxious to know. Jeff was rather loth[31] to tell, but at last the important Discovery was divulged[32]. It was to assist old Keokuk to keep his Harem[33] in order. The idea took, it was concurred by all hands, his muscular and other developments highly eulogized.

John was missing. It was soon ascertained[34] he had gone to board with Keokuk. Some two days had elapsed, John returned to the trading house; much interest was

---

[27] The current town of Selma, also called Stumptown
[28] a person who has more than one wife or husband at the same time.
[29] Fat or overweight
[30] a small piece of tasty food
[31] reluctant; unwilling.
[32] make known (private or sensitive information)
[33] The wives of a polygamous man
[34] find (something) out for certain; make sure of.

11

manifested[35] about his success. John reported rather poor luck. Old Cota a Frenchmen, asked him how much *present he distribute*[36]. It was found out that John was not as liberal as was necessary to succeed well. Jeff Jordan told John he must either come down liberally with presents, or dress himself, trim his hair, and paint so as to outshine all the young braves or give it up.

John was rather stingy, he did not like to invest in trinkets, but if he could afford it he would like to outshine the young braves. A Frenchman offered to do the necessary barbering and painting. Jeff Jordan offered to loan him his new buckskin leggins, Jim Jordan would loan him a new calico shirt, Bill Phelps contributed a very fine new red blanket, other parties gave him their sympathy and kind wishes.

John was much elated, but hesitated at the first step, which was to be sheared and shaved. Oh, only to think of losing that long, beautiful, red-hair!

Cota was ready with shears and razors. Peter Avery said a faint heart never won a fair lady. John seated himself on a stool and said let the harr[37] go, and in a few minutes there was a pile large enough to cushion a chair, then his head was lathered and shaved as smooth as a peeled onion, leaving only a good sized scalp lock on top, cut in the latest fashion; then with some yellow ochre[38] and Vermillion[39] paint the French artist drew the outlines of a rattlesnake coiled around the scalp lock. That emblem so painted is the boldest mark of defiance known among savage nations.

---

[35] display or show (a quality or feeling) by one's acts or appearance; demonstrate

[36] Success with the squaws he had

[37] "hair"

[38] Ochre, is a natural earth pigment containing hydrated iron oxide, which ranges in colour from yellow to deep orange or brown

[39] a brilliant red or scarlet pigment originally made from the powdered mineral cinnabar

While the paint was drying, John ate a hearty meal. Then his vallet de chambre[40] proceeded with his toilet. A turban and breech cloth was furnished by Wm. Avery, and John Collard was completely transmognified[41] into the finest dressed Indian in the nation.

He was truly the observed of all observers. The complimentary expressions used by the traders were numerous and some of them decidedly rich. Jeff Jordan called him an Adones, a perfect Beau Brumell. Some others were more extravagant in their encomiums[42].

It was now late in the afternoon. John left for the village and things became quiet around the trading houses.

It was, however, whispered around among the traders that the fun would likely come to a head by tomorrow morning. John had been informed that it was only the bold and ardent wooer that could win.

He acted on that hint and a little after midnight old Keokuk put John Collard under guard, and as the day dawned, old Keokuk made for the trading houses to complain on the red-headed skin-e-way[43]. The traders were expecting him and were up ready to receive him, and knew from his walk that he was angry.

Phelps was old K.'s big friend, to whom he made his complaint, showing how the young skineway acted.

Phelps now became one of the most busy men on the ground. He fixed the preliminaries for a big scare, and a race, which somewhat mollified[44] old Keokuk. John was sent for and some of the squaws also as witnesses against him.

---

[40] a court appointment introduced in the late Middle Ages, common from the 14th century onwards - a manservant who acts as a personal attendant to his employer.

[41] transform, especially in a surprising or magical manner.

[42] a speech or piece of writing that praises someone or something highly

[43] Young man or boy

[44] appease the anger or anxiety of (someone)

13

The intention of all hands was to have a mock trial, work up John's fears to the running point, give him somewhat the start and make him run rather towards the settlements, but through the Indian village so that all the squaws could see him run.

In those days there was a point of timber of considerable width, near Independent, which grew narrower as it extended up the river, coming to a point before reaching the trading houses. The path or trace run near the river bank, and through this timber along which vedettes[45] were

---

[45] a mounted sentry positioned beyond an army's outposts to observe the movements of the enemy

placed at intervals near a hundred yards apart, two or three in a place, with special instructions how to act, scare him all that they could, but be sure and not hurt him.

While these preliminaries were being arranged by Peter Avery and a big Indian, the trial had been progressing in the most pioneer style. There was no fictitious Judge or other officers; in short, he was tried by the crowd, consisting of about five Indians for every one white man. Jeff Jordan stood by John as his big friend. Keokuk was the principal witness, explaining by words and gestures how John had acted.

The whole scene was so utterly ludicrous[46] that any attempt to describe it is beyond my power, and therefore the reader must supply the omission in his own imagination. The squaws confirmed each other's statement that none of them had received any presents from John. That established their virtuous intentions beyond a doubt. And finally John himself confessed that he had not so much as offered them any presents. Then Jeff Jordan abandoned his defense, and stepped back, or, rather the enraged young braves crowded themselves between them. Phelps could say no more to conciliate[47] them. In a moment a dozen scalping knifves[48] were drawn and brandished[49] almost in his face; but strange as it may be seem they were all of them on one side of John and none of them on the other side. As some two or three of them were just reaching for his beautiful scalps lock, some one sang out "Run, John!"

He went. The red blanket was seen floating in the air. It fell to the ground and John was forty yards beyond the blanket and at least forty feet in advance of all his pursuers.

---

[46] so foolish, unreasonable, or out of place as to be amusing; ridiculous

[47] stop (someone) from being angry or discontented; placate; pacify

[48] a knife similar to a butcher knife used by the Native Americans to scalp their victims. Originally was a stone knife before the English trade.

[49] wave or flourish (something, especially a weapon) as a threat or in anger or excitement

The traders and Indians gave a simultaneous shout, and such a shout as no language can describe. John was going down the old trace. One Indian was near the river bank - another one right in the path. They both drew their scalping knives and made for his top-knot. This made him turn to his left hand. They joined those already in pursuit with an exulting[50] yell. They soon reached another picket post, where two or three Indians went through the same maneuver, turning him still further to his left, and with another exultant yell they also joined in the pursuit. Then the whole woods were full of Indians, all yelling. But the prairie was open. After passing beyond some willow bushes near the lower end of the prairie he had fairly changed his course and was running northwest towards the Indian country.

Many of those in pursuit had been fairly distanced already and abandoned the chase. The first ebullition[51] of joy had died away among the traders and things were nearly quiet.

Then a solitary Indian voice was heard away across the prairie rather in the direction of Tollman's house, saying something to those in his rear that were still in pursuit. All eyes were turned in that direction; John Collard becomes visible with Indians still in pursuit; we count them one, two, three, and all told fifteen with scalping knives in hand; the sight is most beautiful as their bright blades glisten in the sunshine; there is a considerable space between John and the foremost Indian; that distance gradually increases. This race was so much more than

---

[50] show or feel elation or jubilation, especially as the result of a success
[51] a sudden outburst of emotion or violence

any one had heretofore anticipated, all eyes are intently gazing; not a word is spoken for some minutes; the gap is still growing wider. The national reputation of the natives is now at stake; their swiftest braves are being fairly beaten on their own ground in sight of their own people. As the braves settle down to the work with a will, still losing ground, John suddenly raised his left hand and threw his red turban high in air, the sunshine reflected from his shaven pate, his beautiful scalp lock still standing erect it was electrical. A simultaneous shout broke forth from Indians and traders alike; for a time all of them were perfectly happy, their cup of bliss was overflowing and without any alloy[52]. John is doing well. Let him run whilst I philosophize.

Happiness, what is it? What is happiness to one is not happiness to another. The Jew expects to be happy only when he reaches the New Jerusalem, where the streets are paved with gold. Some lazy Christians do not think of happiness until they have reached a state of futurity, as described by Watts:

Where congregations ne'er break up and Sabbaths never end.

Then, happiness operates quite differently on different people. Those traders were perfectly happy for the time being. Phelps would lay down, roll over and laugh, then jump up, look intently for a while, then drop down, roll over and laugh again, and kept doing so alternately. Most of the men would stand up, leaning slightly forward, with arms akimbo[53], occasionally spring two feet from the ground, with a yell, without being aware that they had all moved and then settle again into the same attitude.

John and his pursuers were near a mile distant and opposite the trading houses and have run near a mile while we have

---

[52] An alloy is commonly a substance added to improve a character of metal. In this archaic usage, it means whisky to provide stamina.
[53] with hands on the hips and elbows turned outward.

17

been philosophizing. And John has already done what I have seen many an old buck do when, hotly pursued by wolves, he has turned rather short to the left and is now making for the river. Although the foremost Indian is not gaining on him, those far in the rear, running on a shorter circle, or, as a farmer would say, are taking cross lots, seem to be gaining very fast, and, as they are all approaching the same point, the race is becoming too exciting to confer that perfect state of bliss that the traders had just been enjoying.

John has just reached the timber, and unexpectedly to him, about the middle of Old Van Caldwell's brush fence. It was a very high brush fence. John sprang to the top, a brush gave way in such a manner as to fasten one of his feet; he exerted himself manfully; as his foot became loosened, the brush broke, and he dropped down several feet in the midst of the brush fence.

Then those Indians in pursuit sent up a yell of exultation[54] that was heard for miles around.

The traders and all the Indians started at once for that place.

The Indian that had been foremost in the chase seemed to give out; he was barely able to speak low as the others came up in succession, but he vigorously motioned them forward. They scrambled over the brush without stopping to look and made for the river bank, but John was not visible.

At the place he had fallen through the brush there was a log that had been chopped some three feet from the ground, only cut on one side and pushed over and brush piled on to make the fence. It retained its position and afforded John an excellent hiding place, and he was there quietly

---

[54] Rejoicing or Triumphant elation

ensconced[55] whilst the Indians were hunting every place but the right place.

The traders with a mass of Indians were coming from the trading houses; the Indian that had been foremost in pursuit went towards them looking for tracks, as there was a little newly fallen snow on the ground. He met the crowd, reported the situation, and the hunt became general, but neither white man nor Indian could look anywhere near where John was hidden.

The scouts circled round; they all met at the upper end of the turnip patch, and declared that he must be hid somewhere in that brush fence. They all congregated at that end of the fence nearest the mouth of Soap Creek. Some of them were placed on the look out, but all of them took positions on the upper side, leaving the lower side, next to Iowaville, without a single picket. Another detail of their stoutest men commenced tearing away the brush fence. Even that was a sight worth seeing. The short string was cleared; they turned the corner, and the game was sprung; but John had full sixty yards the lead of all, and the chase was again resumed with renewed vigor. The yelling was most terrific, but not equal to that of an hour previous. The scene was exhilarating; it was glorious, but not equal to the morning performances. John is still gaining, and that is glory enough for our side. We all feel happy, but it is not such bliss as was enjoyed an hour or two previous. Indeed, such happiness cannot be known but once in a lifetime.

The way was clear, and after running about three miles the Indians gave up the chase, completely exhausted. John slackened to a common lope, and as he passed old Patchett's place, afterwards known as Philadelphia, he looked back occasionally, but maintained his own jog trot down through Bentonsport and Farmington. Both these towns had just been laid out. He did not slacken his pace

---

[55] establish or settle (someone) in a comfortable, safe, or secret place

19

until he reached the point where his brother-in-law lived, about a quarter of a mile below Croton. It was now about half-past three o'clock, and dinner was just ready. He ate a moderate meal, crossed the river, passed Sweet Home, and, as he afterwards expressed himself, "lumbered" for the settlements in Missouri.

It was a well known fact that Wm. Phelps or Peter Avery could outrun any Indian in the nation fifty yards, and that Wm. Avery or Jeff Jordan could beat any of them seventy-five yards. But it took John Collard to beat all of them from one jump to seven miles, and then keep on running. After about three weeks absence he returned to Sweet Home, with a pair of new pants, and an overshirt made from coarse bed-ticking. His hair had grown nearly half an inch, but the scalp lock still stuck up prominent. He stayed around a year or two afterwards, but never seemed to enjoy life as well as he had done before he distinguished himself at running. When he went to horse races and gave an opinion on the running quality of horses, some one would slightly infer that his opinion should have weight from his own well known capacity for running. The last that I ever heard of him, he was near Saint Charles, Missouri, and the owner of two good race horses, followed horse racing as a business, and said he considered that his best "holt."

William Phelps is still living at or near Lewiston, in Fulton County, Illinois; still fat and hearty, and has changed but little in those thirty-six years that have elapsed since that great race was run.

James Jordan still lives on the ground at Iowaville; is getting to be an old man; has forgotten some things, but there is still some Jim Jordan in him yet.

T. Jefferson Jordan lived several years on Soap Creek, and in 1850 was preparing to go to California. He had been having the measles[56], stirred out too soon, caught cold, and died suddenly.

McPherson went back up the Missouri amongst the wild tribes.

Henry Netherton and both the Frenchmen followed the Indians to Kansas, where they all emigrated in 1844.

Wm. Avery went to Kansas shortly afterwards and still remains there. He was wealthy, but lost his property during the war.

Peter Avery, who was a good looking but almost beardless boy at that time, I believe, still owns a portion of the land over which the great race was run. He has, however, spent several years in Kansas. He was here some three or four years ago, still hale and hearty, with a long flowing beard as white as an angel's wing.

The Indians, where are they? At that time so full of life and fun. Nearly all have gone to the spirit land, and may they find it a happy hunting ground.

In connection with the above I would observe that this same ground, Iowaville, in 1818 was the scene of one of the best contested battle fields anywhere in the West. The Iowas on one side, the Sauks and Foxes and the other side. It lasted a whole day. The Sauks and Foxes were completely victorious. The Iowas abandoned the country and the Sauks and Foxes became the owners. I have heard many an old Indian boast of deeds performed on that, to them, glorious day.

---

[56] highly contagious disease that caused between 3-4 million deaths before immunization in the US. By 2016, the America's claim it has been eliminated here.

Early Settlements

*In THE DAILY GATE CITY on NOV 20, 1875, A.W. Harlan
tells about some early settlements and settlers in the area.*

At Home, Nov. 13 1875

Eds. Gate City: I have noted in the Dollar Monthly (which
I believe is published at the GATE CITY office,) in the
October number a reward offered for certain information
relative to certain early settlements in several localities,
and herewith proceed to contribute my small stock of
information.

Fort Madison, in October, 1834, had but two settlers, old
Dick Chaney and Nathaniel Knapp. Both of them were men
that required considerable elbow room, Ft. Madison not
being large enough for both of them, where several
thousand persons now live quietly together. Peter Williams
and Mr. Kenneday had small improvements a little below
the present town site.

Captain James White was the only occupant of Montrose in
the spring of 1834, and had some eight or ten acres of
prairie land broken and planted in corn. He lived in quite a
respectable hewed log house. But in June of that year
Lieut. G.H. Crossman, of the United States army, by the
orders of the then Secretary of War, selected it as a place
for a garrison, and proceeded to erect thereon what was
called Camp Des Moines, since known as Montrose. A man
whose name was Murphy was the first soldier that was
mounted on a wooden horse[57]. Please refer to General
Parrott, of Keokuk, for further particulars. I could give
many incidents. A sketch of James White, of the keel

---

[57] A torture device similar to a saw horse where the person is seated straddle
of the device for a certain amount of time, sometimes with weights tied to
the legs.

23

boat[58] Bronthes, was published in your paper some years ago.

Alexandria, Clark County, Missouri, was first settled by Lewis Kinney, in the spring of 1835, and was the sole occupant of the place in that year. He left in 1836, and his cabin was occupied by John Dedman for the next two or three years as a tavern, and a small man by the name of Death kept a warehouse. This was all on that piece of 35 acres known as the Wilcox fraction, which forms the front of the town, though in the summer of 1833 Francis Church had laid out about 160 acres in town lots immediately west of this fraction and called it Churchville.

It was not until 1838 that James Mitchell laid out Alexandria on an adjoining fraction of land lower down and including the Wilcox fraction in Alexandria. On the morning of September 13, 1834, there was no person living within five miles of the place. I have occasion to remember the time, as the afternoon of the 12th was windy and the waves sunk the little ferry flat. Henry G. Stuart, a man well known in Hancock County, Illinois, and Lee County, Iowa, wished to cross the river but could not, and lay down at night amongst the grape vines and mosquitoes, and on the next morning swam his horse beside a canoe across the Mississippi, and I crossed at over in the same way. My recollection is distinct even to the number of mosquitoes Stuart killed at a single stroke of his hand on his mare's neck; we counted them and there were just 55.

Lewis Kinney was an old man, the father-in-law of John R Wilcox, and poor in worldly goods, having broken himself in mill building on the Wyaconda about two mile from LaGrange, Missouri. Refer to R.E, Hill at Alexandria.

The following particulars as to Nauvoo are written from memory, after a lapse of more than forty years, and are only impressions made in part by conversation with those

---

[58] a shallow narrow or cigar shaped cargo boat designed to haul goods up river by pole.

24

people that occupied the place before it was named Venus by Elick White, a son of Capt. James White, and when it had been re-christened by Hodgkiss and Gillett and called Commerce, and also from visiting the Saints during their occupancy, when it was changed to Nauvoo.

As near as I can recollect from various statements, it must have been about 1828 that Capt. White, Hezekish Spillman, Joseph Lemery and a man whose name was Gouge, and probably Isaac R. Campbell, now of St. Francisville, Mo., moved there together in a Pirouke[59] or Pea Rogue, consequently those coming together would bear even date in settlement.

Appanoose, or thereabouts, was first settled by Jothan Clark, Wm. Clark and Peter Gillis. They jointly kept a wood yard, and sold out to Amaziah Doolittle and Edward White - P. Gillis says, in the year of 1827.

Gillis is still in good health and lives near San Simeon, San Louis Obispo County, California. Jothan Clark died near Hamilton a few years ago. Wm. Clark is still living in Clark County, Missouri.

---

[59] "Pirogue" French for a hollowed out log canoe (Pea Rogue).

Crittington Forquerean - A domestic Scene.

In THE DAILY GATE CITY on Mar 21, 1872, A.W. Harlan tells about Crittington Forquerean's problems with drinking.

Crittington Forquerean, I believe should he entitled to the honor of being the first real settler on the Des Moines, within the bounds of Iowa, though several made claims and settled thereon near the same time. Crittington Forquerean made the first claim above the Half-Breed line, and afterwards sold his place to Jonas F. Denny - the same on which James Rice resides at present. His next claim was just below the mouth of Indian Creek, which he sold to Charles Davis. This is at present owned by Dibble. His next location was about one and a half miles above Farmington, on the opposite side of the river, and his fourth location was about a mile above Bentonsport. That place was purchased by your humble servant, and is, I believe, occupied by a Mr. Burton at present.

The next place of which I have any certain recollection of his living was just below Portland. That place, I believe, he sold to Samuel Holcomb. The next place he settled was out in the prairie, a little northeast of Iowaville, where he remained several years.

Old Crit, as we called him, was a Virginian[60] by birth, though raised in Kentucky. He came to Missouri at an early day, and lived not far from Louisiana. His father had once been wealthy, but lost his all by investing in a spurious[61] land title, so common in Kentucky,.

The subject of this sketch was a little over six feet in height, and of dark complexion, a long nose turned well up at the point, and at the time he came here 1833, must have been nearly fifty years of age, though he appeared much older. He had rather a pale, cadaverous, and wonderfully wrinkled face.

---

[60] a settler from Virginia

[61] not being what it purports to be; false or fake.

27

His rather remarkable appearance was occasioned by dissipation[62] and gerrymandering[63] in his younger days. He had a tolerably plump face and digestive capacities almost equal to an ostrich. He was fond of gambling, especially the game of old sledge[64] or Seven Up[65], and has been known on many occasions to sit and play at cards for two days and nights without eating anything whatever. But he must always have plenty of bad whisky to drink, then his appetite would become ravenous and he would indulge in eating to his utmost capacity. At last he became dyspeptic[66] and no wonder.

And after such excesses he would have what he called bad spells. He had them frequently say 2 or 3 times every winter and for many years. At such time he wanted all his family around him and as many sympathizing friends as he could get. He also had in his speech the most confirmed lisp[67] that I ever knew any man to have. That particularly lisp of his seemed on such occasions to give his uncouth explicative's is a charm that is hard to communicate in a written article so the reader when pronouncing any word Old Crit they have spoken, well please do this best lisping.

I saw him have one of those spells once.

But a little family scene that I shall try to give was narrated by one Henry Plummer who had went out that evening to try to court the daughter, with poor success, however.

Old Crits' wife's name was Priscilla. His son Willis was about nineteen years, and Stephen some fourteen years of

---

[62] a descent into drunkenness and sexual dissipation

[63] Manipulating voting districts to benefit one party

[64] Card Game similar to Pitch without bidding – High, Low, Jack, Game

[65] Card Game similar to Pitch without bidding – High, Low, Jack, Game

[66] having indigestion or consequent irritability or depression

[67] a speech defect in which s is pronounced like th in thick and z is pronounced like th in this

age. The place was his home about half a mile from Iowaville and at the time about 1841 or 42.

Old Crit had been drinking and gaming something more than ten days and nights, went home, and I shan't say how much he ate. He soon said "Prithy, I feels mighty bad," and, placing his hand on his stomach, groaned, "Oh, I feels mighty bad," and laid down on the bed. "Marthy, Marthy, my daughter, where are you?" She answered, "I am here." He then inquired for his son Stephen, who had just gone to bed, not upstairs, but up the ladder in the Attic. Old Crit, notwithstanding he was trying to die, called out, "Stephen, my son, come down and see the last of your poor old father." Stephen came down. "Where is Willith?" Stephen replied, "Over at Iowaville, gambling." "Stephen, go tell Willith to come home and see his poor old father die" Stephen went. Willith was losing, so he came immediately; but, instead of coming into the room where his father was, he climbed up at the end of the house on the outside, where be had some large pins driven into the logs, so as not to disturb his mother when he was out late at nights. Priscilla had been busy heating old pieces of Indian blankets in hot water and holding them on his stomach as well as she could. Stephen came into the room, and Old Crit enquired; "Where is Willith?" "Gone up in the loft to bed."

Crit--"Willith, my son, come down and see your poor old father die."

Willis replied, "Dry up, dad, there is nothing ailing you, only you have been eating another peck of sour krout." His mother replied that he had not been eating krout, as it was all gone, so come down and see your father; he is mighty sick. Willis said, "Dry up, marm, G-d d-n it, if dad han't eat krout, he's been drinking up all the buttermilk, then."

Stephen then went up the ladder to coax Willis to come down. Willis said, "D-n you, Steve, show your head again and I'll break your noggin," and Steve subsided.

Crit-"Willis, my, son, I say, come down end see your poor old father die."

Will-"Dry up, dad, G-d d-n you, you could not die if you tried."

(Here old Crit. done some keen cussing, once more urging Willis to come down and see him die.)

Will, after some hard swearing, told his father that God Almighty never had, anything to do with him, and that the devil[68] was not near ready for him. Old Crit raised from his bed, seized a butcher knife, started up the ladder, saying: "Willith, you or I, one, dies this night." As he got into the loft Willis had sprung out at the window, went in, below, and sung out, "Where are you, dad?"

Crit-"Hunting for you, G-d d-n you."

Then old Crit. went down below, while Willis went out doors and up his pegs, called, "Hello, dad, where are you now?"

Crit-"Still hunting for you, by God. Willith, you or I dies this night;" and again he started up the ladder, but the exercise caused him to vomit most copiously, most copiously indeed. That relieved old Crit. He laid down and soon fell into a quiet sleep, and in a few minutes more Willis was snoring loudly, and all was again quiet in the pioneer's home.

Old Crit went to Kansas about 1853 or '54, and at last made a fortune making and selling claims, and then died at almost four score years of age.

[68] The Devil is the primary opponent of God, the tempter

Iowa Missouri Border Issue

In THE DAILY GATE CITY on May 10, 1888, A.W. Harlan gives the other side to the attempt by Missouri to move the Iowa/Missouri border north.

The Other side of the Clark and Lee County Border Difficulty as Told by an Iowa Man.

A.W. Harlan, an old settler residing at Creston, Iowa, writes to the Burlington Post an account of the early war between Missouri, and Iowa over the disputed boundary line between Clark and Lee Counties. He claims that the statement which he gives has never been published, and they do not make a very favorable showing for the Missouri side. His version is as follows:

Some of our tri-state old settler orators occasionally refer to the Missouri and Iowa war, and always in a joking manner. The animus[69] and origin of the said Missouri war[70] was with a few land speculators that had made money on the half-breed tract that only made them land sharks. Wm. McDaniel, of Palmyra, Mo. , was the principal mover in the matter. Now if they could establish the rapids in the Des Moines River at Keosauqua as the northern boundary of Missouri it would naturally extend the area of the half-breed tract, thus giving the speculators about four full townships of land or 92,160 acres; even at the low price of five dollars per acre it would come to almost half a million dollars, all of which amount was to be wrung[71] from the poor man who wished to cultivate the soil. The state of Missouri sent a corps of competent surveyors and took the latitude and longitude of the rapids at Keosauqua, and run a line from thence near Wescottswell, and crossed the Des Moines below

---

[69] hostility or ill feeling

[70] a short squirmish between Iowa and Missouri over the boundary and taxes of that area concerned. It came very close to being an all out war. Sometimes called the Bee War.

[71] Past tense of **wring**- to squeeze or twist especially so as to make dry or to extract moisture or liquid – get everything possible

31

Pittsburg. There they raised a mound and placed some charcoal in it. From thence they run west to the Missouri River, 243 miles, placing some charcoal in mounds at the end of every six miles, thus as they said, permanently establishing their northern boundary. This was done in the summer of 1838. I have been trying to give what has been heretofore the unwritten part of the controversy. From that time on for several years the halls of congress and the legislatures were full of the controversy, up to the time of the final decision of the supreme court of the United States, and the planting of the iron posts at every five miles on the old Sullivan line[72]. I am without exact dates, and will only say about 1839, the county court of Clark County, Mo. , ordered the collection of taxes on the said disputed tract, and hence the war. The governor of Missouri had ordered out about ten thousand troops, and about two thousand had already rendezvoused[73] at Waterloo. Martial law[74] was proclaimed and enforced to some extent. Wm. Phelps, an Indian trader, had a small lot of goods sent from St. Louis to Churchville, now Alexandria. These goods were detained by ...order of Col. John Dedman. And Phelps came down to see about the matter, and in the course of the investigation, it is said, old Bill Phelps knocked some of the "claret'" from the colonel's nose. I never heard any person that was present call it blood. Negotiations between the hostile parties had been in progress. The men assembled in Waterloo had become restless, almost mutinous, and their whisky had give out. Some one proposed putting Couchman on a box to address that assemblage, and it was done. I have heard that address highly spoken of repeatedly. That it was fearless and to the point, and shortly after the crowd dispersed and the war ended.

---

[72] The Iowa/Missouri line today (was the border between Indian Territory and Missouri when surveyed)
[73] To meet or come together at an agreed time and place.
[74] military government involving the suspension of ordinary law.

Common Little Indian Fight

In THE DAILY GATE CITY on Nov 17, 1869, *A.W. Harlan tells about an Indian attack on Bill Phelps at the home of Mr. Bedell.*

In a fight there is generally two parties, sometimes there is more. Let me proceed to introduce them; Bill Phelps, who does not require an introduction anywhere in Iowa, and indeed in but few places in the western country, because in the west there are more than one hundred thousand men that, could call him by name on meeting him.

At the time of which I am writing he was about twenty-four or twenty-five years of age, with not a wrinkle on his face, though some people then called him "old Bill Phelps." In height he was about five feet eight inches, and weighed two hundred pounds, a perfect blonde, having light colored hair and blue eyes, full, rosy cheeks, mouth rather small, teeth perfectly white, a musical voice that some persons might call rather feminine, but I have often noticed, in a large crowd, where men were noisy, that I could hear his voice ring out distinctly above all others. His neck was rather thick, he but seldom buttoned his shirt collar, would ride all day with his breast exposed, with the thermometer at or below zero. He was not an Indian trader, and it was a well known fact that there was not an Indian in the Sac or Fox nations that could beat him running fifty yards. He had the appearance of being fat; he was fleshy, but it was rather a redundancy of muscle that enabled him to move as quick as any man. He was always ready for a horse race, a fight or a foot race, and either of the three were nearly alike sources of amusement to him. The Indians called him Che-che-pe-qua.

I have seen many Indians, could call them by name, have tried to study their characters, (if they had any) but I never

33

could understand their hearts. An Indian, when sober, and not excited, is dignified and generally quiet; but give him the proper quantity of bad whisky, and in a few minutes he becomes a Devil incarnate, and then in a little while longer there is nothing left of him but a drunk Injun.

Now the question that has bothered me, is this: whether the devil lay dormant in the Indian, and was only developed by drinking bad whisky, or was the devil in the whisky that the Indian drank, and as I have but a small smattering of theology or metaphysics, or chemistry, the question puzzled me. The Indians have uniformly decided that the devil was in the whisky. My theology teaches me the devil is a spirit, and therefore I have long since concurred with the Indians, and had little to do with whisky.

One cold morning in December, 1832, Bill Phelps was passing with a friend, and called in to Mr. Bedell's cabin. Here he met two Indians that; by some means, had got just enough bad whisky to make them fond of adventure. There was one other Indian, with his squaw, a party to themselves, that were duly sober; with Mr. Bedell's whole family, in a room 12x14 feet square, with poles, or joists, so low that a man six feet in height could not stand erect, though Phelps could stand up straight.

Now with Phelps sitting on a stool, jovial as usual, with the two Indians squatting before a broad fireplace, and all seemingly quiet and comfortable, we have the parties ready for a small fight.

But just let me premise that Phelps had been out as an interpreter with the Government troops in the war the summer previous. One of these Indians recognized him, and eyed Phelps rather "affectionately." This made Phelps all attention; he heard him say to his comrade that he had lost his squaw and two papooses in the war and he meant to have revenge. Though spoken rather low, and in their own language, Phelps understood that about as well as they did themselves; of course he was on his guard, and as the

Indian rose to his feet, having previously slipped his hand under his blanket and grasped the handle of his butcher knife, he struck; but Phelps, being a little the quicker with his fist, knocked him sprawling, and seizing his rifle that set near by, placed the muzzle against his head and snapped the trigger, but luckily be had discharged it a few minutes before he came in, and had not thought to reload his gun. He dropped his rifle instantly and, as the loft was rather low and the room too much crowded for good fighting, he seized the Indian, threw him out at the door onto the frozen ground on his back, and sprang with both feet on the Indian's breast. The knife had fallen from the Indian's hand, and all done so quick that no one thought to interfere.

About this stage of the game the other Indian came to the rescue, tomahawk[75] in hand. Then it was Bill Phelps' turn to run a little. He turned round the corner of the house so quick that the Indian could not strike him fairly, and, as he run, drew a knife from his belt, and at the last corner of the house confronted the Indian. Each of them seemed to know the necessity of making a sure lick. Several motions were made. The tomahawk was the superior implement. The Indian knew it, but he also knew that the blow must be well directed or his heart must soon feel the cold blade of the knife. He made a step to one side to make a sure blow. In that moment Phelps sprang near six feet and jerked the tomahawk out of his hand. Not, however, without some resistance, for the Indian as quick run for his gun. But the sober Indian had knocked out the priming and spit in the pan. Mrs. Bedell had seen him do it, so there was no one to look after but Phelps, as all the arms had been hidden away in much less time than it takes to describe the scene, except what Phelps had. The sober Indian wanted Phelps tied, but just then I should not cared about undertaking the job, and in a few minutes more it was not necessary.

---

[75] a stone axe developed by the Native American Indians, later was made of metal and became one of the popular trade goods in the fur trade.

There was no blood spilt; but the Indian that begun the fight was badly hurt in the breast; however, he lived a few months, and had the credit of dying a natural death.

The fight being over, I will now close with this partial description of Phelps. He was always a moderate eater and a very moderate drinker. He loved a joke dearly, and card playing as well, although I never knew him to banter a poor fellow; but, if solicited, would play for money always, and what he won he always kept, no odds what a fellow's wants might be.

But then he had some redeeming traits. One of them was, the poor wayfarers that called at his house, and their name was legion[76], he always invited them to eat of such as he had, and if a poor fellow took only two or three meals there was no charge. But if he went to laying round sponging, he would set him to work a few days, then pay him off and let him go.

Phelps, like other Indian traders, moved once or twice every year. They were compelled to be at the point that the Indians might designate as winter quarters, after taking their fall hunt. This must account for Phelps living in so many places on the Des Moines. At the time of that little episode in Phelps' life, in the jam[77] of the fence where the Indian's gun sat, there was some little seedling apple trees some two or three feet high. They were afterwards planted out into an orchard[78]. There were five bearing trees twenty-five years ago. Nearly one half of them have died with old age. The balance, now standing, are large old trees.

The Indians, I believe, have all gone to the happy hunting ground. Wm. Bedell left for the spirit land twenty-four

---

[76] Meaning many, as the group of demons Jesus drove out of a man, 3000 men in a Roman army

[77] Where two segments of a split log fence cross over each other

[78] in settling the Northwest Territory, settlers were required to plat 50 apple trees and 20 peach trees to prove their settlement permanent and keep their land grant.

years ago. Nancy Bedell was stout and hearty until within four years. Bill Phelps is now, perhaps, in 1869, more than sixty years of age, and, even with his temperate habits, is growing gray, and the writer hereof feels old age creeping on.

Elm Bottom

William Bedell - the First Settler of Elm Bottom.

In THE DAILY GATE CITY on NOV. 21, 1869, A.W. Harlan gives some physical characteristics for William Bedell. The Elm Bottom was an area that today is called Sweet Home twp in Clark County, NE Missouri and located south of the Des Moines River east of Athens and west of St Francisville, MO.

A full description of him would be beyond my powers. No person ever knew him. Although a man of considerable ability, he never even begun to know himself. He was a unique specimen of humanity; a curious compound of virtues and vices, utterly incomprehensible, if not incompatible.

In height he was about five feet nine and one-half inches; complexion light, whiskers a little sandy, a high broad forehead, mouth rather large, with a large blue eye that I have looked at in vain for the bottom. It twinkled with every change of feeling, and with any one else would have been a true index to the soul. With him it was an unfathomable mystery.

Now let me acknowledge myself beat, as almost every person has been that ever had anything to do with him.

It is only by giving incidents in which he was an actor that any person can form a correct idea of him, and not even then.

History should be truthful, for false history and lying tombstones have covered a multitude of sins and been the bane of the past as well as of the present generation. And should this short sketch happen to offend any one, let me apologize by assuring them that no offence is intended. Then, if they will wait until I have been dead twenty-four years and think me worth naming, please try to draw the sketch as honestly as I am trying to do this, and

Would the powers some giftee gave us
To see ourselves as others see us,
It would from many a silly blunder free us.

First Sermon in the Elm Bottom

In THE DAILY GATE CITY on Nov 21, 1869. A.W. Harlan describes the first sermon in Sweet Home by Joseph Howard.

Was by Joseph Howard, in March, 1836, a minister of the sect known as the Cumberland Presbyterians[79]. He had come in and settled within the present bounds of Lee County, Iowa, on the east side of Sugar Creek timber, and not far from where Warren Post office is at present. He was a large, stout man, rather corpulent[80], with a full face, and deep furrows in his cheeks. He had been raised on the frontier of Illinois, had been a soldier in the U.S. Rangers, and loved good liquor[81]. He was rather illiterate, but preached a sermon about level with the comprehension of his hearers, and generally done his level best.

The meeting was held in Josiah Roberts' cabin, in Sweet Home. The room may have been sixteen feet square, containing all his household goods and a large family of children. With the hearers, I can truly say the house was well filled; the preaching was earnest if not eloquent; the singing was tolerable; the closing prayer truly fervent and the religious services were over. But the most interesting portion of the meeting was still to come. A small keel-boat, containing some emigrants and their goods, landed just at the mouth of that small brook about that time. The preacher must stay and get some dinner, and while this was being done Bedell went on to the keel-boat and got some whisky to drink. Now whisky operated on Bedell very quick; that is, sufficiently to evoke a devil that would make a drunk Indian ashamed of himself; but it took a large

---

[79] the Presbyterian Church was primarily a Lutheran Reformation of Scottish settlers governed by an assembly of elders. in the US. Most areas of Scottish immigration were Presbyterian in faith.

[80] Fat, paunchy, chubby, overweight

[81] a drink of any alcoholic beverage, usually whisky in the pioneer days.

amount to floor him. On the keel-boat there was a man who seemed to be a hand - a large, two-fisted fellow, who had but little to say. Bedell put himself in his favorite attitude, that of a panther just about to spring on to his prey, and with a grin, looking the fellow in the face, gritting his teeth, grunting "yah-yah-yah, ain't you much scared?" The fellow struck at him; some one warded off the blow, and told him that was old 'Squire Bedell. He said 'Squire Bedell had better get off from that boat, and some of the rest of us took his advice as well as Bedell. But when 'Squire Bedell got on to the bank, the shrugs of his shoulders, his grimaces, his attitudes of defiance were inimitable[82]. We all looked at him, and so did the two-fisted stranger, but devil a word did he say, and after eyeing him awhile, quietly walked on shore, and with his open hands slapped both sides of Bedell's face, and as quietly walked back again. I looked at him and thought I should like to know his name, but I did not care about such an introduction as 'Squire Bedell had. Those two little slaps started the tears from Bedell's eyes most copiously.

He left and started for the house. The preacher had started for his horse, which was in a stable on the river bank, without any kind of a lot about it. The manure had been thrown from the stable and thoroughly worked up by the hogs, and as Bedell expressed it himself, was a perfect "lob-lolly[83]," three rods wide and four inches deep. They met about the middle. Bedell, with outstretched arms, clasped Howard, gave him an affectionate hug, and with tears still streaming from his eyes, dropped on to his knees, saying in a solemn tone, "Brother Howard, will you pray for me?" Howard had on his Sunday suit of home-made blue-mixed jeans, (I can see him yet.) He looked at his pants; he looked at the "lob-lolly," but came down on his marrow bones. He prayed both audibly and eloquently, and for a good length of time, but when the Amen came they

---

[82] As good or unusual as to be impossible to copy; unique.
[83] a thick gruel; mire, or mud hole

both rose. Bedell said, "Brother Howard, you have made a powerful prayer, and you are a powerful big man. They have got some d-d good liquor down at that keel-boat; come along with me and I will treat you; then I shall want you to help me whip a great big two-fisted rascal that struck me a little while ago." Then the preacher began to comprehend the situation. I can even yet see the conflicting emotions in his countenance. At last tears came to his relief. Those were tears of genuine chagrin.

Thus ended that portion of the performance. The reader will bear in mind that Bedell's tears were tears of pain. As for tears of repentance, I am not aware that any were shed at this our first meeting in the Elm Bottom.

The keel-boat left its moorings and Bedell left for Sam Thompson's doggery[84]; the preacher bridled his horse, and the writer hereof assisted old Josiah Roberts to ferry the preacher and his horse over the Des Moines.

Nearly all early settlers on this river have seen a kind of ferry boat improvised by placing a platform on two canoes; but in this case we only lashed a small canoe on to the side of a large one to keep it from turning over, and had the horse stand up in the big canoe.

---

[84] US slang. A disreputable drinking establishment

First Settlers in the Elm Bottom

In THE DAILY GATE CITY on Nov 7, 1869, A.W. Harlan tells about the first settlers in the Elm Bottom.

The name is almost forgotten, but it was, or is now, that pretty scope of farming land immediately on the Des Moines, below the town of Athens, in Clark County, Missouri.

The first settlers were Wm. Bedell and __ Peevler, his given name I have forgotten. Then came the two families together. Where Peevler settled, the land is now owned by Wm. Clark, and we have no memorial of him, save that a little creek still bears his name. Not so with the Bedell family. Although Wm. Bedell was a very dissipated[85] man, when sober he had tolerable abilities. But his wife, Nancy Bedell, was one of those women designed by nature as a pioneer of civilization. They came here in the year 1830. Bedell's cabin stood on the river bank a little below where Charley Buckner now lives. Here for two summers they raised corn in peace and beat their hominy in a hole on the top of a walnut stump. I think some of the roots are still there.

This primeval mill was made by taking a long springy pole, placing it horizontally on some saplings or wooden forks, the small end being generally eight or ten feet perpendicular over the stump to which a smaller pole is attached by some linn bark; in the lower end of the smaller pole there was a split;

---

[85] overindulging in sensual pleasures, whiskey & women

45

a hickory withe around the end prevented it spreading further; the point of an iron wedge was inserted in the split and the mill was ready. True, it run by elbow grease; but the reader will bear in mind that it was a great saving on the back, as the operator only had to give vigorous downward jerks, the head of the wedge cracking some corn and the spring-pole raising it up ready for another jerk. The fine portion would pass through a meal sieve, and made good corn cake; the coarser portion was made into hominy. Then the women sometimes boiled corn and grated it on a grater, an implement so recently used that I shall not attempt a description.

In 1831 old John Boone settled among some sugar bushes just in the lower edge of Athens - now grown to be quite large trees - and cleared a small field, just where the business part of Athens, on the hill, is at present - 1869. Old Mr. Wainscott settled the same year in the bottom below the mouth of Peevler Creek. All was peace, and things looked lovely.

But in February, 1832, came the great ice freshet[86]. The ice blocked at the cut off below St. Francisville, and commenced gorging. The river filled with ice, spread over the banks, flooding the country, various depths, from six to fifteen feet deep, up as far as Bentonsport.

Mrs. Bedell had only time to reach high land with her children and most of their household goods, until the ice knocked down their house, the ice piling up where the house had stood about fifteen feet high.

Then Mr. Bedell thought he had learned about the right place to build, so he erected two small cabins away back near the upper corner of the old orchard, got under shelter all right; but then misfortunes but seldom come single-handed. It was so in their case. The Indian war, known as

---

[86] Breakup of ice caused by spring thaw causing flooding

46

the Black Hawk War[87], broke out in Illinois, with some hostile demonstrations west of the Mississippi.

The authorities in Missouri, advised the most exposed frontier settlers to retire back towards the older settlements. They all left their homes along the Des Moines and fell back to Cottonwood Prairie, near where Canton, Missouri, is now situated. But the war seemed to be confined entirely to Illinois and Wisconsin, and corn-planting time was approaching. A number of the men returned and planted corn, part of the men scouting through the country while others worked the corn. But Bedell returned with his whole family - Nancy and their seven children.

Now, some gentle reader may exclaim, what a foolish trick, but let me remind you that at that day there was no such thing as organized charity anywhere in the West and those people had never been beggars, and the feeling of self-dependence and self-reliance is what most distinguishes us as a people.

Mr. Bedell watched for Indians while son John ploughed[88] corn. But his family would want for clothing when winter should come. So Mr. Bedell went up nearly opposite where Farmington is now situated, to assist Wm. Jordan in cutting- saw logs to raft to St. Louis, to procure necessaries in time to come.

Nearly all frontier settlements have had false alarms, which are full as bad sometimes as real danger. Let us have one on paper.

Christopher Wainscott and James Boone looked more for Indians than what they did at work. Some hogs got frightened at them and run. They got frightened at the

---

[87] Blackhawk war 1832, US Military attacked Blackhawk's tribe when they tired to re-settle on native lands where they found their native burial grounds plowed and bones exposed by the settlers.
[88] spelling for plowed, outside the US and Canada; same with plough vs. plow

hogs, and they run. This occurred out back of Athens. They come down to Mrs. Bedell and reported Indians near by. Mrs. Bedell started her son John for his father late in the afternoon. Night overtook him; he got lost before he found his father, and wandered most of the night through the woods, not daring to hollow[89] for fear of the Indians. At last the boy come to the wise conclusion to lay down and wait for daylight, and when daylight come he soon found his father.

Boone and Wainscott agreed to remain and watch for Indians near Mrs. Bedell's cabin, until the next morning, or until the boy would return; but when morning came Boone and Wainscott were not to be found. They always said that they staid until dawn of day. If so they must have made good time, for they reached Fort Pike[90] but little after sunrise, and that was fifteen miles distant from the starting point.

Now, gentle reader, you may imagine Mrs. Bedell's situation. Her son had not returned, as she expected, and everything seemed to indicate that both had been killed, and if so her time to be scalped must soon come. But she did not run, nor did she take much time for weeping. She had two ponies that had been concealed in the brush, brought by the little children, while she packed up nearly all her worldly goods and tied all on the ponies, and, with a piece of charcoal, wrote on the door, "We have gone to Rutherford's." Then put on her five little children and started; had went but a little way until she saw her boy coming. He said his father was alive. She then stopped to shed a few tears (tears of joy). Bedell soon came with a canoe, down the river, and took the oldest girl with him in the canoe down to Fort Pike. That was a block house, not yet built, though just begun on the bank of the Des Moines, where St. Francisville now stands.

---

[89] Yell loudly to be found (holler)
[90] Fort Pike was constructed at St. Francisville, MO

48

Nancy Bedell continued her march over the prairie, and, as Boone and Wainscott had reported the situation, volunteers were called for and a detail made to go and hunt them up. They were just ready to start when Nancy Bedell came down the hill in full view, with her two pack horses and loads of little children, safe to the Promised Land, and were welcomed by a shout of joy from those pioneers that made the welkin ring[91].

They raised some corn, but did not ask alms of any one, and when winter came the whole family were assembled in their little cabins, cheerful and hopeful.

---

[91] Loud shout rejoicing or celebrating

First Jury Trial on Elm Bottom

In THE DAILY GATE CITY on DEC. 1, 1869, A.W. Harlan tells about the first trial on Elm Bottom.

The first jury[92] trial in the Elm Bottom occurred in the spring of 1836, and not far from the time of our first meeting. Wm. Bedell was the acting Justice. The case was against James Smith, for vagrancy. The complainant was Lloyd Rollins, rather the wealthier man in the neighborhood.

The complaint was made out in due form, charges set forth, subscribed and sworn to.

The warrant had been issued, served, and the parties were on hand, a jury summoned, and all ready for trial.

The reader will bear in mind that said James Smith that was being tried for vagrancy in Missouri, was at the time living in Iowa, as well as the Constable, Nathaniel Dews, who served the process. I would further premise that said Smith was rather a lazy, worthless fellow, living on a claim immediately above the Missouri line. It was rather a pretty piece of land, on which Rollins looked with longing eyes.
It was generally believed, though never proven, that said Smith held that claim for Frank Church, with whom Rollins was not friendly, and hence the suit for vagrancy. Perhaps I had as well explain some further, that under the then laws of the State of Missouri,, the man proven to be a vagrant was sold out as a slave to the lowest bidder; that was, to the person that would take him and work him for the shortest length of time, not exceeding six months, to pay the expenses of his own prosecution.

The jury was empanelled[93] and sworn; your humble servant was on that jury, as well as Joe Benning, M. Couchman

---

[92] trial by jury, a panel of peers.
[93] Jury members were selected

and others, for it took nearly all the men and part of the boys to make a jury.

Frank Church appeared for the defendant, and suggested a want of jurisdiction, as Smith did not live in Missouri.

The Court overruled that motion, then turning to the statutes of Missouri, he read a recent act of the Legislature obliging all attorneys-at-law to first procure a license before being allowed to practice law.

Col. Church wanted to know, as the man was being tried for vagrancy, if he could not appear as his next friend.

'Squire Bedell informed him that himself and the jury would proceed to try the case without any of his assistance.

Church, of course, had to succumb. His eyes flashed, and the scowl on his countenance showed that his dignity was offended.

Frank Church looked at that jury. He thought Rollins owned that jury, and had a strong lien on the Justice; he had no hopes for Smith.

The trial proceeded. Several witnesses were examined for the prosecution. The cross-examination was mostly done by the jurymen; many important facts were elicited relative to the case that I will not try to repeat. I took items myself, on paper, and remember the summing up. Smith kept a small oak trough in his house in which he kept his meat. It was not proven that it had ever been entirely empty; he had killed a hog of his own the previous Fall that weighed over 100 pounds, and had bought about 50 pounds of pork of Nathaniel Dews; and although his family had been out of meal, they had not been out of boiled corn. It was also proved that during the previous winter he had killed and eaten as many as three Coons!

The testimony closed; the justice, witnesses and spectators withdrew, and left the jury to themselves; we compared notes; generally agreed; soon fixed on a verdict, and I believe it was on my motion that Melgar Couchman, at that time only a boy, but long since known as Judge Couchman, of Illinois, was made our foreman. He wrote our verdict in nearly these words: "We, the jury, &c[94], &c, after a patient hearing, are of the opinion that the complaint has not been fully sustained by the evidence in the case, and that therefore we find that said James Smith is not a vagrant, within the strict meaning of the law."

The Justice looked a little disappointed, but received the verdict quietly, as we had no whisky on hand.

Col. Church looked more cheerful, approached the Justice, and asked, in a rather subdued tone, if he could then address the jury.

'Squire Bedell told him he might, as they were already discharged.

Frank Church was a small man, with a remarkably keen eye, and an uncommonly heavy beard, hanging down over a large ruffled shirt bosom, and could put on more dignity and style, I think, than any little man that I have ever met. He stood erect, raised himself on his tiptoes, and came down on his heels, so as to make some noise to attract attention; then raised his right arm slightly; then opened his hand, raised his arm considerably higher, and gently waving his hand in the air, and much as to say, attention! ye common mortals, Colonel Church is going to speak. The crowd was all attention: He stroked his beard with his left hand, hem! Hem'd a time or two and the words came forth. "Gentlemen of the jury" - and again he stroked his beard - "I thank you for your verdict" - again he stroked his beard, hem'd. "Gentlemen of the jury, you have given a righteous decision." Here he paused some time, then said: "By your decision you have established the fact that a man has a right to catch and eat coons whenever he d-d pleases."

---

[94] Their abbreviation for etc. or etcetera

Thus ended the first jury trial. We cleared Smith, but it was a mighty tight squeeze; so tight that no one blamed Rollins, the Complainant.

First Wedding in Elm Bottom

In THE DAILY GATE CITY on DEC. 1, 1869, A.W. Harlan tells about the first wedding on Elm Bottom.

The first wedding in Elm Bottom occurred at the house of William Clark; the parties were John Goodwin and Elizabeth Purdom; the time was September 1836, and the couple came from a little above where Keosauqua now stands. A few words and only a few may be necessary in explanation, as it is only, the wedding with which we have to do just now, but the whole scene, as told by the traveler, Bill Smith, would be decidedly rich. He could relate all the particulars with a feeling of pathos not to be expected from any other individual. The parties were of age; had been promised some months; the bride's parents were opposed to the match; the young people had been planning a runaway match, when Harlan appeared on the stage and volunteered his assistance, and at the first effort carried off the bride in a canoe; got the groom on board about where Games' tanyard[95] is at present.

The river was pretty well up, the sun had almost set, and it was pitch dark before we reached Bentonsport. But Harlan, young as he was, had steered several boats to New Orleans, and he steered that canoe. John Goodwin paddled that canoe as an expectant groom might be expected-to have paddled. By a few minutes after ten o'clock, we reached Wm. Clark's residence, a double log cabin in the Elm Bottom, 25 good miles. Harlan introduced the couple, then went for 'Squire Bedell. He came with the Missouri, statute in hand. He told one that his heart began to fail him and he must have some whisky first before he could solemnize the marriage. I waked up old Nathaniel Dews and started him to Sweet Home for a half gallon of liquor. In the meantime

---

[95] an area of a tannery set aside for the operation of tanning vats

'Squire Bedell searched the statute carefully to find some form for a marriage ceremony. There was none to be found; true there were forms for summons, for subpoenas and executions, with fee bill attached, but none seemed to be appropriate for the present occasion. At that time I had not yet learned the meaning of the word fail, so your humble servant committed to paper the best marriage ceremony that he could manufacture, impromptu, handed it to the 'Squire. He read it to himself; called me to one side and pronounced it d-d well done. The liquor arrived; the 'Squire imbibed about half a pint; he studied that ceremony carefully a few minutes, then took nearly another half pint, then called me to one side and said he had got it by heart. Now said he, as soon as I take another dram[96], then get up the young people before me. It may as well be stated on this occasion I acted in the double capacity of groom and bridesmaid. I squared around the chair, and joined their right hands. The ceremony proceeded; it was closed; they were pronounced husband and wife; but almost in the same breath, Bedell said "d-d it all, I don't see why the hell it should scare me so." And by half after eleven o'clock I had them put to bed and left them alone in their glory.

I saw 'Squire Bedell afterwards on some two or three occasions perform the marriage ceremony; he always cussed himself for getting scared. On one occasion, he had scarcely pronounced them husband and wife, until he brought down his right foot on the floor with a force that would have moved weak nerves, exclaiming, "the hell and damnation, I don't see why it should always scare me so."

---

[96] A dram is equivalent to about ½ Cup (.469 Cup)

Isaac Gray

In THE DAILY GATE CITY on Dec 10, 1869, *A.W. Harlan tells about Isaac Gray.*

Isaac Gray, One of the Early Settlers of Elm Bottom.

The writing of that name calls up a thousand memories. I shall, however, only name a few incidents, barely sufficient to fairly illustrate his character.

At the time he come here he was about thirty-four years of age. This was in the fall of 1832. He was about five feet eight inches in height; his hair might be called black; he had an eye that I could not say whether it was blue or hazel; he stood erect with a square forehead; his jaws were a trifle too large for perfect beauty, denoting a trifling preponderance of the animal over the intellectual faculties; his teeth were perfectly sound and double all around, and occasionally, when under the influence of liquor, would bite an eight-penny nail in two. His muscular development was also most perfect, with not an ounce of superfluous[97] flesh about him. His breast was full, indicating an excellent pair of lungs; his health was admirable; his capacity for endurance was wonderful. But his capacity for resisting temptation in any form was weak; his love of strong drink was wonderful, but in his sober moments his regrets and remorse was felt keenly. Good resolves were made, but they only lasted until he again met temptation. I have often felt of his muscles in those early days, and told him that if he would only keep sober, that he was yet good for one hundred years of good health.

He appreciated a good joke, and often tried to be facetious[98] himself.

---

[97] Unnecessary, especially through being more than enough.
[98] treating serious issues with deliberately inappropriate humor; flippant.

For about ten years he and Squire Bedell were almost constant companions, and I think they were both of them on a spree[99] about one third of the time. Their many tantrums[100] and practical jokes I shall pass over, for the citizens of every little town within a hundred miles of here has witnessed their sprees, and Isaac Gray loved to be called Ike.

The horse has been the constant companion of man for at least three thousand years, Alexander had his Bucephalus and McDonald his Selim, and old Ike had his horse Comet. He was a chestnut sorrel, about sixteen hands high, and hard to beat six hundred yards, as that was his distance. I have often known him to stand hitched to the horse-rack two days and nights at a time without a bite to eat, and I think on a few occasions all of three days.

Old Ike generally rode with an old bridle, by which Comet would stand hitched quietly, never breaking loose, and when old Ike would get on his back to go home he would regulate his motions so as to keep his master in the saddle, and it was no uncommon thing, that, after this horse had stood hitched a whole day and night without feed, Isaac would get to bragging on his horse, make up a race, run him and win the race; but in such cases he generally had to stand hitched at least twenty-four hours longer.

On one occasion Isaac had been on a tare[101], down in Farmington, for some two or three days, and the people generally wanted to get clear of him. Old Squire Craig and some others set themselves to work and got old Ike onto his horse Comet. The river was well up-that was a rise of something over ten feet. They flattered themselves that if they could get him over the river they would, at least, be

---

[99] a spell or sustained period of unrestrained activity of a particular kind.
[100] an uncontrolled outburst of anger and frustration, typically in a young child.
[101] On a spree, drinking, winning, or ?

rid of him for a while. They had the ferry all ready to ferry him over gratuitously. With a good deal of work they got old Ike down to the ferryboat. He thanked them for their kind intentions, but he could inform them, by G-d, he kept a boat of his own. He rode old Comet into the river, reined him down stream, and kept on near the middle of the river as far as they could see him. That was about two miles. He came out all right at home, where Athens now stands, a distance of five miles.

Now be it known that amongst the early settlers there was a good many men besides old Isaac that were fond of staying rather late at night where bad whisky was to be drank, and men of that stripe generally rode gentle, worthless old tackeys. It was a favorite amusement with Isaac to turn their saddles wrong end to and help them on, to see some fun, and with old plugs nothing serious had ever occurred.

But in order to illustrate a case somewhat out of the usual line, I am compelled to introduce a man of quite a different stamp.

J.J. Benning came and settled out back of Sweet Home, in the fall of 1834, and was the first settler out on the edge of the prairie. He was a duly sober man; did not mix in their frolics[102], and on one or two occasions reprimanded Isaac and some others rather sharply. This, when Isaac was sober, he knew to be rights but when he got on a spree he viewed it in rather different; he had long sought for an opportunity for retaliation in his own way. The time had come at last.

Bedell had started a grog shop[103] in Sweet Home. Isaac and other congenial spirits were on hand. The eggnog was just ready, and Benning, for once and once only, so far as I know, and that is now thirty-four years, got completely

---

[102] Cheerful playing happily
[103] A low class bar room

fuddled[104]. He had rode a large, young iron-gray horse, that would run away every good chance he got, and balk whenever he pleased.

Isaac was very friendly and kind to Joe when Joe got tight, and so when Joe got ready to start home, Isaac was very helpful. Joe knew that he needed some help, and received it kindly. Isaac helped him into the saddle, and then gave him the bridle and started the horse.

In order to understand the situation, the reader must be informed that Isaac had turned the saddle the wrong way; that is, the other end to, and as he handed him the bridle, had put the bits under the horse's tail, where the crupper[105] should have been.

The horse became frightened and made a lunge down hill. Benning pulled hard at the reins, spoke gently, said "whoa Jim," about twice, and the horse was out of hearing around that little hill, down a steep bank, across Cedar Creek, and up the other bank, going for home at break-neck speed, with Benning on his back, with his face towards the horse's tail, occasionally saying in a firm, mild tone, "whoa, Jim;" but the horse did not stop. He took the road for home, up, that steep hill, with Joe Benning still pulling hard at the reins, saying "whoa, Jim."

The horse reached the top of the hill, and went about a quarter of a mile towards home. Here he balked; had a spell of kicking up behind and before. With all his kicking up he could not hoist old Joe; but here the horse had changed ends, and thought this operation was something new, took fright, and ran as fast back towards Sweet Home, down that hill. Here he took a turn up the river, through the woods and over logs - the path went at that time back of Clark's field - and jumped into Clark's yard, and stopped, almost exhausted with fear and running, trembling all over,

---

[104] confused or stupefied, especially as a result of drinking alcohol.
[105] a strap buckled to the back of a saddle and looped under the horse's tail to prevent the saddle or harness from slipping forward.

60

Joe still saying. "whoa Jim." Bill Clark helped Benning off the horse and into his house and took off the saddle, but the horse held a death grip with his tail on the bridle bits, but when the bridle was taken off, he came to his senses. So did Joe Benning by the next morning, and both went home quietly.

Who is it that has not read of Tam O'Shanter's race on his gray mare, Meg? He was nearly scared to death, and so was his mare, and he was right end to, and had a bridge across the creek, while Joe Benning only kept saying gently, "whoa, Jim." And what child is there in these United States that has not read of John Gilpin's famous race, near London, in England, that forever immortalized his name? He only run on a plain turnpike road, and tried to carry some liquor in bottles, swung on each side, and broke his bottles at that; while Joe Benning carried his liquor in his hat, safely, over a path in the dark, where Gilpin could not have stuck on ten minutes.

The whole secret is this: In their cases each of them had a poet at hand to immortalize them in verse. Joe Benning's case was different. Here, after the lapse of a third of a century, only part of the particulars are given in prose.

Isaac was something of a mimic. He could mew like a wild cat and squawl[106] like a panther. He was having a spree up at Lexington, above where Bonaparte, stands at present. One poor fellow had been hanging around, spunging liquor all day. He had a mortal fear of wild beasts, but a greater love for bad whisky, and his hankering for whisky had predominated over his fear until late at night. But go home he must. He started; so did old Ike, and by a shorter path he headed him off. Isaac mewed like a wild cat. The fellow was so frightened that his legs refused to do duty. He stood still. Isaac sprang on to him, bore him to the ground, scratched him on the face, and tore off his old clothes. The fellow screamed a few unearthly screams, and if he raised

---

[106] Alternave spelling of squall - cry noisily and continuously.

a hand or foot, that moment the wild cat's claws would literally enter the flesh and hold it down.

He swooned: he thought he died. The wild cat was making a meal of him; nibbling at his carcass, and occasionally tearing with his claws. He done the dying so well that even old Ike became a little alarmed, and ceased operations for a time; lay down by the fellow, felt over his heart a long time before the beating was perceptible, but at last all was right. Isaac scratched a few leaves on to him, squatted near him, done the necessary snapping and a little genuine purring, and left him in the happy land of Canaan. But he soon awoke, and found himself still here below, on dull earth. The use of his limbs came to him at last; he went home, and for months, and perhaps for years, he firmly believed a catamount[107] had attacked him. Indeed, the signs left on his body inclined some of his friends to be of the same opinion.

After Isaac had been spreeing about thirty years, the spring of 1850 come; he must have been more than fifty years of age; myself and others was with him on the plains, going to California; whisky was not so plenty and Isaac kept duly sober from the Missouri River to near the further side of the great desert beyond the sink of the Humboldt and near Carson River. Such campaigns is where men learn to know each other truly.

Isaac walked every step of the way, with that long, trusty rifle of his on his shoulder, always ready for use, night or day; indeed he was the only man that I saw on the whole route that was always ready for work or an Indian attack at all times.

Here I might give some interesting reminiscences, but this article is already much too long. One little incident and I will taper off.

---

[107] Cat of the Mountain - Cougar

Isaac left the teams in Carson Valley,, and started to walk over the Sierra Nevada Mountains. He went over and through those large banks of snow where Fremont left the howitzer, crossed over the back bone of the Sierra Nevada, went a few rods to where flowers were blooming. Here he met the tempter[108]; he drained a bottle, and when I found him was taking a snooze with his trusty rifle beside him.

I took that empty bottle in my hand; some emigrants may remember a high ledge of basaltic rocks to the right of the road; I climbed to its highest pinnacle, placed the bottle, mouth down, with several small rocks to keep it in position, and left it as a memorial for the future traveler, just where that angle was afterwards made in the Eastern line of California,.

I went back to Isaac, I stood, I reflected a long time, I placed him in an easy position, and left him in the arms of Morpheus[109].

When Isaac reached the mines the old enemy still followed him there. He spent some four years in the mines, dug some gold dust, but the tempter was always on hand to rob him. He returned to his old home, and after some two or three years found his rest in the grave yard.

I have dropped this subject abruptly, hoping an abler pen may, at some future day, finish the sketch, and draw a moral from his faults.

---

[108] Devil - a person or thing that tempts
[109] Greek God of Dreams

Trip Down the Wabash and Mississippi

In THE DAILY GATE CITY on Aug. 28, 1888, A.W. Harlan tells about the spread of Cholera up and down the Mississippi in 1833..

A.W. Harlan told yesterday of a trip down the Wabash and Mississippi Rivers in 1833. He started in a flatboat[110] about 300 miles up the Wabash and went as far as Natchez in thirteen days; there he met the cholera[111] and his men refused to go farther with him. There were twelve boats at the wharf with about forty men on them, and in two days nineteen of them were dead from cholera. He sold his stock of flour, whisky and pork, also his boat and took passage for New Orleans. Arriving at that port he found the cholera abating and the yellow fever[112] raging. There was no city organization, the officers of the city having been carried away by the scourges. Boats that were arriving from the gulf were unloading many children whose parents had died on the voyage. They wandered around the town until cared for - some of them he says were sent out as slaves to the plantations.

---

[110] usually a one way vehicle to haul goods downriver. Flat bottom up to 20' wide and up to 100' long.

[111] Cholera is an acute diarrhea disease that can kill within hours if untreated.

[112] Yellow Fever is a deadly viral disease caused by mosquito bites. Can be deadly since no cure is known. Can cause liver damage, internal bleeding, kidney damage etc/ Was considered one of the most dangerous diseases in the 18th and 19th centuries. Vaccination is required if traveling in many countries of the world.

Boating on the Des Moines

In a letter written in 1900, A.W. Harlan tells about boating up the Des Moines River.

I have been thinking, and have concluded to begin with my first experience of boating on the Des Moines River, and mention facts as they occur to my memory, admitting that I have forgotten many things. My first experience was the little keel-boat Black Hawk, and then with the Union. Both of these boats belonged to the Phelps'. This was in 1835; I do not think I did any boating in 1836. It was in September, 1837, that I shipped from Sweet Home, MO, by the steamboat S.B. Science, Captain S.B. Clarke, a lot of goods which was landed just below Keosauqua, Iowa. The Science then went up to Iowaville and returned.

She was the first steamboat to Iowaville; but in the same fall, 1837, I shipped a lot of goods on the Pavilion, at St. Louis. The boat was commanded by Bill Phelps, and we had for passengers, the celebrated Indian Chief, Keokuk, and about a dozen other braves, returning from Washington City[113], after having sold that small strip of land.

My goods were landed below Keosauqua, and the boat went on up to Iowaville, taking the Indians to their

---

[113] Washington, DC

destination, which was near that place so the Pavilion commanded by Captain William Phelps was the second steamboat to reach Iowaville, in 1837.

The Pavilion was up in the spring of 1838, and I think that Phelps went up as far as the mouth of Coon River[114]; but of this I am not certain. The S.B. Science was sunk near Bentonsport, but she was raised again and left the river.

There was a man by the name of Captain Cash, who made several trips with a keel-boat, trading and freighting. There were others also, engaged in the same way, but I have forgotten their names. Henry Bateman, engaged in boating stone coal from Farmington to Quincy, Ill. in 1836, in keel-boats. He built one or more old fashioned flatboats that he loaded with coal for Holmes, of Quincy, Ill. The coal was unloaded to run the mill there, and the boats were loaded with flour for New Orleans.

[114] Raccon River in Des Moines

68

It was on the bottom of one of these boats that we pioneers congregated to celebrate the Fourth of July, and the birthday of Wisconsin Territory, in 1836. There were about three hundred of us. We clubbed together and bought of Bateman, one barrel of whisky and put it in care of James Jenkins, to deal out at his discretion, free! After a time he concluded that he was of no use, and asked to be relieved. Then the rest of the day any man who wished, drew and drank when he pleased! There was but one man in the entire company who seemed the worse for the free whisky. Of all that little patriotic assembly, I know of but one besides myself now living. His name is Amos Hinkle, and possibly John Bedell, of Red Rock, Iowa. I want the forgoing incident to have a place in Iowa history - for we could not do it to-day!

Now as to your main question as to the "name of the boat which carried up the soldiers and supplies in 1843" I cannot answer; but can tell something about the steamboat "Ione," of which inquiry has been made.

In 1834 and 1835, Sol and Pierce Atchison lived on the bank of the Mississippi River, at a point that would now be about the upper corner of Nauvoo, Illinois. Pierce Atchison at that time was on the river, in the summer of 1838. He seemed to have charge of two steamboats, known as the Glaucus and the Ione. Late in the fall of 1838, the Ione struck a snag near Clarksville, Missouri, and sunk. She was still there the last I heard of her.

In February 1839, I was with Sam Atchison, a nephew of Captain Pierce Atchison, then on his way to meet his uncle at St. Louis,, who was bringing up a new steamboat he had ordered built on the Ohio River, which proved to me that he had abandoned all hope of raising the sunken Ione near Clarksville. I do not remember ever to have seen any other steamboat Ione.

As to the list of steamboats sent me I can say but little. The General Morgan was commanded by Granville Hill. The

Light was built at Bonaparte by Richard Cave and Commanded by him. She was capsized by the wind and sunk near Hannibal, Missouri. Mr. Alfrey of Farmington, Iowa, owned and ran a keel-boat about 1843. The steamboat Newton Waggoner, commanded by Newton Waggoner, made one or two trips about the same time. Captain McPherson was on the river at a later date, but I do not remember the name of his boat.

As to flatboating, Ed Manning and the Steeles had a flatboat built by Samuel Morton down at Rochester, Iowa,, and towed it empty up to Keosauqua, where it was loaded by Manning and Steele with about 60 tons of bulk pork. This was in the spring of 1841. I was duly installed as captain at Alexandria. I put on in addition ten tons of barreled beef and piloted the boat safely to New Orleans. In the same spring Hugh W. Sample built a small boat near where Kilbourne now stands, and ran seven tons of pork to Alexandria, near the mouth of the Des Moines, and shipped the cargo to Pittsburgh, Pa. , on a steamboat.

I think it was in 1847, the year of the great famine in Ireland, that I ran several flatboats loaded with corn to St. Louis. At the Athens Mill, the dam was eight feet high. The mill owners had a wooden lock 25 feet wide, but the gates had been broken out by the ice. Now to run the chute left open was rather a precarious business. A failure would have been almost certain death, but by good management and a little experience as a guide I made the passage a number of times and thought very little about it, until the danger was passed.

While on the subject of early boating on the Des Moines, I think it well to mention the fact that up to 1840 I had not noticed that the banks of the river were washing away; but in the year 1850 the people generally began to observe it. The great flood of 1851 killed the willows and the wash became greater, and continued until about 1890, on both banks of the river. And now, for about nine years, it has been filling in on both sides even faster than it washed

70

away, and the willows have grown up surprisingly. It is now no more the beautiful river that charmed the stranger in early days.

I am now in my 89th year, having been born in 1811, not far from Cincinnati, Ohio, among the Indians, my birthplace being on the Indiana side of the Ohio River, so you will not wonder that memory is failing me.

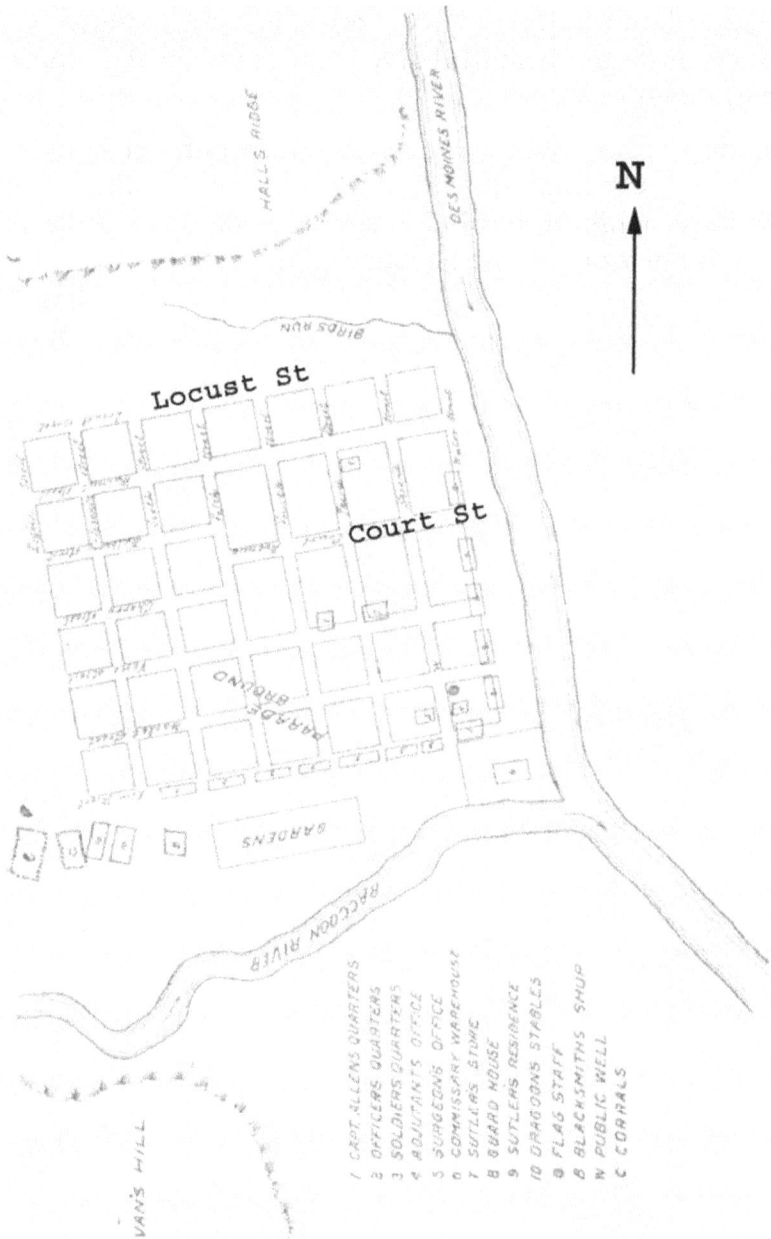

The 2nd Fort Des Moines - the beginning of Des Moines, Iowa –
Now downtown. 1st Fort Des Moines was at Montrose, Iowa

Early Times in Iowa

A letter written by Hawkins Taylor in the "Brighton Sun" on July 20,1878, tells about daily life and ministers in the community

To see the name of my dear old friend L.B. Fleak, at the head of your paper as Editor, brings to my mind most vividly recollections of the days of old, days - never to be enjoyed in Iowa again. The State has now an entire new organization; then no one locked his door at night and in warm weather it was left open, but if shut, the latch string[115] was always out. If a stranger came within your door, he got a part of what you had and if a new settler wanted to raise a cabin, his neighbors turned out and raised it for him; if he got sick his neighbors planted and plowed his crop; if he lacked a few dollars to pay for his land at the Land Office, they let him have it without interest until he could pay it back. When a family wanted to go back to see their friends in "Elenois[116]" or Indiana, they took their ox or horse team and went.

---

[115] a string that is attached to the door latch. Can be placed on the outside so the door can be opened from the outside, or pulled inside to lock the door to outside visitors.
[116] Illinois

73

They took with them and cooked their own provisions, and at the end of six weeks or so, would all come back, fat as bears. When the Methodist circuit rider[117] came around, as he did every few weeks, or the hardshell Baptist[118] held forth, the population turned out to hear them. If provisions were scarce and it was a busy time with the "craps[119]," it was not uncommon for the men to take their guns along, and after the preaching, provide the next week's meat.

Circuit Rider

There was no time spent by the women either in meeting or after, in criticizing the bonnets and dresses seen in church. There was no hierogriphical[120] sort of singing, keeping you all the time in distress for fear some one's throat would rip. In these good old days, it was earnest, good old hymns or songs that made you feel good all over. If there was a wedding, there was no junketing[121] around to show off the fine bonnet and "such" things. When the wedding was over, the groom took his wife to their cabin, and she cooked their dinner for them, and they went to work to till and replenish the earth.

If a settler proved not to be of the true metal, his neighbors told him to go, and he went. The principal court of that day was a court that never made mistakes, and allowed no appeal, and the only court that ever existed that rogues and ruffians feared; but that court has been abolished. In place of the old log cabin, and the out-hanging latch-string, is the fine mansion, and the strong locks and bolts, to keep out the increasing civilization. In place of the circuit rider and

---

[117] an early form of Methodist preacher who traveled thought the US on horse back and preached in open fields to the settlers.
[118] Primitive Baptist Church that was against the missionary spirit, Sunday School, preacher salary, theology schools, temperance societies, etc.
[119] Slang for Crops
[120] Totally understandable
[121] taking an excursion for pleasure.

other preachers, preaching in groves, where benches and shades had been prepared, and where families from a distance were taken to welcome homes and dinner furnished them by neighbors near by, so that they could come back to afternoon service. Everybody tried to have the preachers go home with them, and then all denominations joined in attending those meetings, ever ready to feed the strangers.

Now, there would be a terrible lack of, Christianity if there was not a grand church, with cushioned pillows, only open to the stranger by the suffrance[122] of the owners. The first thing you meet is the collection basket. The music would scare any animal on earth that never heard it before.

The preacher reads a sermon that he or some one else has written. The women examine each other's bonnets, and the new way of frizzling the hair, and calculate where they can get something that will beat everybody else the next Sunday. The old men will do a fair share of sleeping, if the minister reads well, the young people will telephone[123] each other and in conclusion, the women will sweep.; the door steps with their dresses, and that ends that day, but nary stranger is taken in and fed.

---

[122] Alt spelling of sufferance - enduring of hardship, affliction, etc.; allowance of wrong doing

[123] Hard to believe, but the telephone was invented in 1876, Bell Telephone Company was founded 7/9/1877, by 2/17/1878 phone exchanges existed in Connecticut and San Francisco.

During the Fall, Winter and Spring of 1836 and 1837 a Methodist preacher by the name of Cartwright, living in Des Moines County, preached in West Point, on his way to Van Buren County once a week. Rain or shine, snow or sleet, he was at his appointment.

That was a desperate cold winter, and there was no road more bleak and dreary than the one from West Point,, to the timber of the Des Moines River. There were twelve or fifteen miles of open prairie, without a house, and fancy him crossing that prairie in a northwest wind with snow, sleet and rain falling in torrents. It was truly a hard circuit, but Cartwright never failed his appointments, and in all the year did not receive in money what would be the present weekly pay of your leading minister in your fast town.

If all preachers were as self-denying as this man, there would be fewer followers of Bob Ingersoll[124].

The noble self-denial of this one man was enough to stamp as untrue all the infidel[125] theories of all the Bob Ingersolls of the land. How many self-denying preachers could the new civilization produce at this time? At that day there were more hardshell Baptist preachers in Lee, Des Moines and Van Buren Counties, than of any other denomination. With two of these ministers I was quite intimate. Father Bradley who died in Lee County and Father Rowland who was living in Fairfield a few years since, and is probably still alive, He is the last of the hardshells in Iowa, so far as I can learn. They were popular and pious preachers of old time, but would be a great curiosity under the present civilization. They communed with no other denomination. They opposed all Sunday schools, temperance societies, bible societies, missionary societies, etc., and held it to be

[124] A famous agnostic who constantly ridiculed religion.
[125] A person who does not believe in a religion or God.

76

a great sin to receive money for preaching. I have known them to absolutely turn members out of their church for joining a temperance society. They opposed all Sunday laws and all laws for the suppression of vice. They were for years and years the ruling party of Kentucky. No man could be elected Governor in that State that was not supported by that church. For years they ruled Illinois, electing Kingsly Governor, who was a man of powerful mind, but uncultured, and rather prided himself on his not being a "college man." He was their leading minister, and the power of the church died with him. Professor Peck, a Missionary Baptist",, a man of education and great ability, and great in satire, traveled the State over, making temperance addresses, and holding up to ridicule the Hard Shells", and it happened just at this time, a Baptist church in Salem, the hardest town in Sangamon County, (Abraham Lincoln was clerking in the only store in the place at the time) had up two men on trial before the church, charged with being guilty of irreligious acts, the one a most worthy man, living in Clay's Grove, a few miles from Salem, (a strongly Presbyterian community) and had joined the "Clay Grove Temperance Society," the other had got drunk, which was not an uncommon act, and when drunk, got into a fight and got badly punished. On trial the man who joined the temperance society refused to acknowledge anything wrong in the act and was turned out; the other one confessed his fault and was forgiven. Professor Peck told this story in its utmost ludicrous light and in most humorous manner, and it broke the prestige of the Hard Shell church, and Illinois, like Iowa, has buried the last of the sect.

I have said enough for once and more than you will print I fear. I have not said a thing that I intended to say, when I commenced. I intended to say a good deal about Keokuk, L.B. Fleak, Vanorsdal, Hillis, H.J. Campbell, Bill Clark, Charles Moore and other of the early settlers, but will have to do that some other time. When I get to thinking or writing about the old settlers of Iowa, I entirely lose myself and get as wild as our President seems to be just now, but am happy to say is not one of the old settlers of Keokuk, and was never there, but I would be a thousand times happier, if he would listen to, and be governed by the advice of that part of his Cabinet which comes from Keokuk. If he did, we would have a Republican instead of a Democratic executive; Republican appointees instead of rebel ones.

Hawkins Taylor.

She Shot

In the May 17, 1879 edition of "THE GATE CITY", tells of how the Crow-Grant Feud was revived and the ensuing battle between the Constable and Justice of the Peace.

Kate Grant Indulges in Nocturnal Pistol Practice Knives, Revolvers, and Knock Downs A court Under Arrest.

The old Crow-Grant feud, which has been the source of so much trouble and litigation in Van Buren Township, has been revived and a new chapter in the imbroglio[126] is presented - probably the most exciting one that has yet been enacted. It seems that a few days ago Mrs. Grant took up some cattle belonging to Crow, which had invaded her premises, and held them for damages.

On Tuesday night last Crow and another man, supposed to have been a fellow named Beecher, who works for him, went to Mrs. Grant's about the middle of the night and attempted to recover the cattle by stealth. Kate Grant, daughter of Mrs. Grant, discovered them in the act and opened fire upon them with a revolver, firing three and possibly more shots at them. None of them took effect but Crow is reported to have said that the bullets whistled past him and struck the boards in rather unpleasant proximity to him.

On the following day, Wednesday, Mrs. Grant applied to Wm. Shepherd, a Justice of the Peace, to have the cattle taken charge of and disposed of according to law. Shepherd gave instructions to Constable Jim Herron to take charge of the cattle, but the latter claimed that he had no authority for so doing and refused to execute the order. An altercation arose between the Constable and the Justice about the matter in which Herron drew a knife and assailed

---

[126] an extremely confused, complicated, or embarrassing situation

Shepherd. The latter whipped out a revolver, but, finding that he did not have time to cock it, struck Herron over the head with it, knocking him senseless. He soon recovered and renewed the attack, whereupon Shepherd cocked his revolver and leveled it upon his assailant, but a bystander interfered and put a stop to the deadly conflict.

Herron went before Squire Garvick in Des Moines Township, swore out a warrant against Shepherd and had him arrested. Shepherd gave bond for his appearance, was released from custody and there the case stands. The matter will go into the courts we presume and another long siege of litigation in this neighborhood strife will no doubt ensue. We learn the facts from a citizen of Van Buren Township who was in the city yesterday.

Burris City

In the Feb 7, 1897 edition of "THE GATE CITY", copies the Ottumwa Sun article of Aaron Melick about how the lost Burris City Flourished and Vanished.

How Burris City Rose as in a Night, Flourished and Then Vanished.

ITS SITE IS NOW A SANDBAR

Of the hundreds of Sun readers, how many of them know that we have a lost city in Iowa that was once known throughout the length and breadth of the land, as a thing of beauty that promised to be a joy forever? The older citizens living in Iowa in the early '50s will call to mind the many railroad projects that lived, flourished and promised fabulous wealth to the state and untold riches to the people who owned corner lots in many towns and cities that existed in the minds of honest projectors of these enterprises. The state was to be banded with "ribbons of steel," and the iron horse was to chase away forever the Indian, the buffalo and all that sort of thing.

Soon came the surveyors, and among the many promising lines of railroad none took precedence over the great Air Line road from Boston to Omaha and through to the golden shores of California. People of Iowa believed in it. On the eastern side of the state, where they had been building their houses and fences of second-growth cottonwood lumber and making their winter fuel of the refuse of the same timber it was promised that pine lumber should build the houses, and stone coal from Pennsylvania and Ohio should be utilized for fuel at a low price, to be paid for with Iowa bacon and cattle at a gorgeous figure. Many of you remember the great barbecues held along the line of the road as made on the map of the state by the aid of a string. Every town tried to outdo every other town the same as when Ottumwa went into the glucose and broom factory business.

Now we come to the lost city of Iowa. The first railroad line through Iowa was to cross the Mississippi a short distance above the mouth of the Iowa River. In going west to leave New Boston in Illinois, a boom town, and Toolsboro, Iowa, another boom town to the left, thence to Burris City on a promontory "between the two rivers, thence to Wapello, Louisa County; Lancaster, Keokuk County; to Eddyville and thence through to Council Bluffs, IA. Well, we recollect the banquet in the capital of proud Louisa, the table in the court house yard, groaning beneath the weight of the best edibles the land afforded; the whole block covered with an awning made of boughs cut from trees in full leaf. The gay imported and bedizened[127] uniforms of the brass band and the big Dutch man with a huge moustache from Burlington who played a symphony on the bass drum.

Colonel W.W. Garner, Editor Noffsinger and other notables were to explain what a scheme it was to vote a tax to help this great civilizer along and across the state. The meeting was a great success. An immense crowd was present. The enthusiasm was unbounded.

Of the prominent actors on that stage that beautiful summer day, almost all that we remember have passed to the other side where we hope they enjoy their riding in golden chariots or silver vehicles 16 to 1.

About the year 1858, N.W. Burris, one of your smart, go-ahead sort of fellows, with an eye to the future, bought a tract of land on the north side of the Iowa River,, at its junction with the Mississippi, platted it, started a town, and named it Burris City. The proprietor was a man of limited means, but shrewd, enterprising and imaginative. The railroad scheme helped him: himself with pleasing address and a reader of minds, he employed good talent, the best there was to be had and boomed the town and people believed in him. He borrowed thousands of dollars on the

---

[127] Dress up or decorate gaudily.

faith in Burris City. People in that section believed a great city would be built there and invested their money. Burris erected saw and planing mills and started brick yards and within sixty days he and others had erected more than 100 buildings there, many of them substantial structures. This was in the days when eastern capital was seeking profitable investment in the west. One of Burris' agents, C.R. Dugdale, went east; and, oh my! how he did boom that town. He was provided with plenty of money to be invested in advertising and placed it where it would do the most good. He also carried with him several highly colored maps, and innumerable lithographs, giving a bird's eye view of the great City, with its wharf lined with steamboats, the airline railroad, street cars, churches with their spires reaching up heavenward, parks, lakes and drives inhabited by spanking teams and gaily dressed people. Dugdale was known as the financial agent of the enterprise and was well fitted for the position. Through his activity, plausibility and printed adjunct he sold hundreds of lots at big prices to eastern people. Some of them, however came west, took a look at the city, but all invested their money. Lots sold rapidly at $1,000. A man named Dunlap started a newspaper, the Burris City Commercial, a fine appearing weekly, of which our own E.H. Thomas was foreman, and O.G. Jack was the boss job printer. Dunlap was a man of large experience in newspaper work, but was dissipated; he had spent several years in Washington as private secretary to some congressman, and while there, it is said, contracted the habit of drinking too much whiskey. One of the best buildings of the place was a fine three-story brick hotel, owned and managed by the Stafford Bros. It was fitted up in grand shape, with marble floor billiard room, saloon in the basement. On account of the many visitors there it did a large business for four or five months. Ed Stafford was, an old newspaper man, and, as Dunlap was a failure, Stafford was induced to purchase a complete outfit for a daily paper and job office. The material was shipped to Burris City, but the paper never materialized. Many other great improvements, like the daily, died in embryo.

Old settlers in that section know that the land on which the city was being built was subject to overflow. Burris was aware of this but his plan was to grade it up above high water mark, shipping the dirt in on the cars during the winter before the spring rise and that those who had invested would contribute their portion of the expense. Unfortunately for the city the fall rains came heavy and continuous. The Mississippi and the lower Iowa both got on a boom at once in the early fall of the year, a thing never known before. There was from six to eight feet of water on the main streets of Burris City and boats were in demand to save people from drowning. Stafford counted fourteen dead bodies in his billiard room and his cook caught a ten pound catfish in the oven of the kitchen range.

The flood washed away all sorts of embankments, filled wells and cisterns with sand and caused general demoralization among the bean-eaters who had located there. They folded their water soaked tents and uttering curses both loud and deep, left the country forever. Thus died Burris City and it was lost for all time. The founder at one time refused an offer of $300,000 for his interest in the city, but his faith overcame his judgment and he left the site as poor perhaps, as when, he bought it. What few buildings the water left were soon tore down and carted away and taken to other points. Burris went to Colorado and was killed by the Indians.

The last the writer ever saw of Burris City was along some time toward the close of the '60's. We were passengers on the "Jennie Whipple," Captain Campbell's tug, toward the close of the summer about the hour of sunset, when the shadows grow the largest through the dull red cloud and the captain remarked: "I guess we will not stop at Burris City this trip," in reply to an inquiry, "there it is."

A desolate strip of country, largely sandbar, on which rested a stranded keel boat, broken in the back, the planking off, the ribs half buried in the sand, while the buzzards that had been enjoying a savory meal from plucking a cadaver of some sort, of this good staunch steamer as she ploughed her way through the waters of the grand old Mississippi, slowly and regretfully flew away. Knowing the history of the place in its palmy days, the present site gave us a shiver and, with the captain, adjourned to the cabin to take a cup of coffee. Thus you see Iowa has lost a city that has long since passed to dust and dreams.

AARON MELICK

Early Days in Iowa

*In the Dec. 26, 1900 edition of the " Constitution Democrat",
Dr. Salter, Clergy at Congrational Church of Burlington, tells
of early days in Iowa.*

Dr. Salter, the clergyman of longest service in Iowa, delivered, at the Congregational church of Burlington, an address on "Early Days in Iowa," from which the following is taken:

"After being made a part of Michigan territory in 1834, and of Wisconsin territory in 1836, the territory of Iowa was created in 1838, and the first legislative assembly of the territory convened in this city sixty-two years ago, on the 12th of November. A census taken in 1836 showed that in three years 10,531 persons had come to Iowa. In 1838 the census showed a population of 22,859. Pursuant to law by appointment of the governor, Robert Lucas, previously governor of the state of Ohio, an election was held September 10, and the assembly convened in Burlington on the 12th of November.

"That day was a day of great interest in Burlington, to which the people had, looked forward with eager expectation. The territorial legislature of Wisconsin had met here previously, and the people had come from every portion of the country. The prohibition of slavery here which had been enacted in 1820 did not prevent a large emigration from the southern states. It encouraged many to come, who disapproved of slavery, who came, for the very reason that the land was dedicated to Freedom. There were more members who were natives of those states in the first legislative assembly than there were who were natives of the northern states. The whole number of members were thirty-nine, of whom nine were from Virginia, eight from Kentucky, one from Tennessee, one from Maryland, and two from North Carolina, making twenty-one, a majority of the whole number. The New England states furnished five members one from Connecticut two from New Hampshire, two from Vermont. New York furnished four, Pennsylvania four, Ohio- four. Illinois, one, making eighteen. The assembly consisted of a council with thirteen members, and a house of representatives with twenty-six.

Old Zion Church

The council met in the basement of Old Zion church, as it was afterwards called; the House of Representatives in the upper story. Des Moines County had eight members, three in the council and five in the house, a larger representation than any other county. Jesse B. Browne of Lee County was president of the council. He had been a captain in the United States dragoons under General Henry Dodge, and was six feet seven inches in height, the tallest man in the assembly. William H. Wallace of Henry County was speaker of the house. The oldest and the youngest member of the assembly were from Des Moines County, Arthur W. Grimes, 60 years of age, and James W. Grimes, 22. Fourteen of the members were under thirty years of age, three of whom came to high and honorable positions in the subsequent history of the state. Stephen Hempstead of Dubuque became the second governor of the state. Serram Clinton Hastings of Muscatine was a member of six territorial legislatures. In one of which 1845, he was president of the council. He was one of the first two representatives to congress from Iowa in 1846-7, chief justice of Iowa in 1848 and afterwards chief justice of California. James W. Grimes was the third governor of the state 1854-8, and United States senator, 1859-1869.

Such were the men who were called to frame the first laws of Iowa. They gave themselves to the task with vigor and industry and completed it in seventy days. Mr. Grimes was chairman of the Judiciary committee in the House of Representatives, and all the laws passed through his hands. Their clearness of statement, their freedom from verbiage and ambiguity, is largely due to his critical sagacity and judicious revision, in which he had also the assistance and co-operation of Mr. Hastings of Muscatine, who was a member of the same committee. By judges learned in the law that code is to this day held in high honor and esteem. Pursuant to an act of the last general assembly of the state it has been reprinted this year by the historical department of Iowa, under the careful eye of Mr. Charles Aldrich, the accomplished curator of that department. The laws provided for the administration of justice by courts, for roads and ferries, for common schools and academies, for the punishment of crime, for the erection of a penitentiary at Fort Madison, for the establishment of the seat of government in Johnson County, with a provision that 'for three years the sessions of the legislative assembly shall be held in the town of Burlington.

The governor of the territory was a man of high personal character, firm and unyielding in his convictions of duty, and an ardent supporter of education and moral order. With the experience of years and of public service as governor of the state of Ohio, he had an overweening[128] confidence in himself to direct in matters of legislation and entrenched

---

[128] showing excessive confidence or pride.

so much upon the rights, and prerogatives[129] of the general assembly as to bring on a bitter controversy, with a large majority of the members of the assembly. Fifteen of them, who belonged to his own political party, were so indignant[130] at his course that they petitioned President Van Buren for his removal from office. Foremost among them were Mr. Hempstead of Dubuque and Mr. Hastings of Muscatine. Among those not of the Democratic Party, Mr. Grimes was leader of the opposition to the course of the governor. The controversy resulted in an act of congress (March 3, 1839) amending the organic law of the territory and curtailing the governor's power.

"By the action of the legislative assembly the supreme court of the territory held its first session in this city on the 20th of November. During the same month occurred the first land sales in Iowa; at Dubuque, November 5, and in 'Burlington, November 19. Those were occasions of the most lively interest. They attracted a large concourse of people eager to secure a title to their homes from the United States. The receipts at the United States land office in this city during that month were $295,000. The late Gen. A.C. Dodge was register of the land office, and he once told me that, when shipping silver dollars in kegs to the United States sub treasury at St Louis, he employed Mr. E.D. Rand to transport them from the land office to the steamboat.

"In conclusion I shall be pardoned it. I add that it was in the stirring days of that November, on the 25th of the

---

[129] a right or privilege exclusive to a particular individual or class
[130] feeling or showing anger or annoyance at what is perceived as unfair treatment.

month, a few Christian people in this town met in a house then used for a school taught by Mr. J. Parke Stewart, which stood on ground now occupied by the county jail, and organized this church with twelve members, the Rev. James A. Clark, a graduate of Yale college, 1834, who had been sent to Iowa by the American Home Missionary society, the same society that sent me here in 1843, preaching and assisting in the service. He was then stationed at Fort Madison and was invited to remove here, but preferred to remain in our neighboring city. Prominent among the members were Mr. and Mrs. James G. Edwards, Mr. and Mrs. William H. Starr, Mr. Joseph Bridgman, who a few years afterward removed to Muscatine. Mr. Edwards was a native of Boston and son of a revolutionary soldier, who fought at Bunker Hill. He was the founder of the Burlington Hawkeye. His wife, with no children of her own, had a mother's heart that embraced scores and hundreds of other people's children. Mr. Starr built the houses that stand immediately north of the church. He was a classmate in Yale College with the Rev. Mr. Clark. The lives of these good men and women and their associates were incorporated and interwoven with the foundations on which rest our institutions of social and religious order. Let us honor their memory by continuing and perpetuating their work, by advancing the city of Burlington and the state of Iowa higher and even higher in things that ennoble and enrich human life.

'"From a population of 22,859 in 1838, the census of 1890 shows a population of 2,251,899 in Iowa. With such history as we have behind us in the nineteenth century, who shall fix a limit to the progress of the commonwealth[131] in the twentieth century? May those who have entered into this inheritance, and those who shall enter into it, guard well the sacred trust, and make the future history of Iowa one of the noblest chapters in the book of time!"

---

[131] a political community founded for the common good.

In THE DAILY GATE CITY on Feb 26, 1870 A.W. Harlan adds the following:

William Clark., one of the first settlers of Elm Bottom, was truly one of the pioneers of the West. He was raised in Ohio, migrated to the Wabash country, Indiana, in an early day, from thence to Fort Clark, in Illinois,, where near Peoria is now situated; from thence he still came West, and for some years kept a wood yard a little below where Warsaw, Illinois is now situated. He went to the lead mines for a short time and then return to his wood yard near Warsaw. There he married and shortly afterwards moved to Missouri and located and made a considerable Farm on land that at present constitutes a part of the town of St. Francisville, Clark County, Missouri,, and traded said Farm for his present location, being the first place first occupied by Pevler. Mr. Clark moved on to his present home in the fall of 1834, and has now been a widower about twenty-five years.

The Indians called him "Nesholo", signifying twin, he being a twin brother of Jotham Clark, recently deceased, one of the early settlers of Hancock County, Illinois.

He is fond of good liquor and tolerably fond of bad whiskey, has had frequent spells of drinking for at least twenty-five years, but deserves much credit for being sober sometimes for months. People of late years call him Old Billy. He is about six feet high, dark complexion, stout build, still enjoys good health, and looks like he might last about twenty-five years longer.

He says that he has frequently done without bread for more than six months at a time, but at those times he generally had boiled corn or hominy, and like most pioneers, he likes a good joke, even if he should be the butt of the joke himself. He is now about sixty-seven years of age, and has been partially bald for many years. I believe that he has never been a professor of religion.

93

George Jones

*In the Nov. 7, 1877 issue of "THE WEEKLY GATE CITY",
reprints an article in the St. Louis Globe-Democrat by Ex-
Senator George Jones reports on early days in Iowa.*

George Jones

There is perhaps, no public man in the country richer with
reminiscences-political and personal-than Gen. George W.
Jones, of Iowa. Born in Vincennes, Ind., in 1804, and
living subsequently in various States and Territories, and
serving as Minister abroad, he has a career both eventful
and romantic. A reporter , of the Globe-Democrat who met
him the other day was surprised to see him still hearty and
vigorous, his little form as erect as an Indian's and his step
as elastic as it was twenty years ago. Time has acted so
leniently with him that one would scarcely believe that
seventy-three winters have passed over his head. His life
has not only been remarkable for a direct connection with
the development of the great West, but for an intimate
association with the illustrious men who figured
conspicuously in national councils a third and a quarter of
a century ago, and for a variety of personal adventures that
have fallen to few men. When he was two years of age his
father moved to, the village of Ste. Genevieve, Mo. In
1814 he moved to St. Louis, and Gen. Jones' earliest
recollections are of the far-Western town that has since

grown to be the great metropolis, of the Mississippi Valley, possessing over a half million of inhabitants, and rich in trade and manufactures. In 1821 young Jones was sent to Transylvania, University, Lexington, Ky., where he was intimate friend of a number of youths whose names have since become famous.

MEETING JEFF DAVIS.

Jefferson Davis

Among these was Jeff Davis, between whom and General Jones there has always been the warmest friendship. "Jeff, was a very handsome boy," said General Jones, "and one of the most brilliant and learned young men I ever knew. We were chums together at College, and I regretted very much when he received an appointment to West Point. I remained at Lexington until I finished my course. At twenty-seven years of age I left Missouri and went to Iowa to regain my health, which had become much impaired by close application to the study of law, which I pursued under the tutelage of John Scott, of Ste. Genevieve. I settled in a part of the Territory of Michigan, now called Iowa. I built me a log cabin in the wilderness and led the rough life of a pioneer. One night, about dark, a horseman rode up to my gate and hallooed[132]. I went out and the traveler asked if he could stay all night. I replied that my

---

[132] cry or shout "halloo" to attract attention

accommodations were poor, but I supposed he could stay. I asked him where he was from and where he was going. He replied that he was from Galena, and on his way to Fort Dodge. "Why," said I, "my friend, you are clear out of your way. This is not the road from Galena to Fort Dodge." I lived out in the wood and not near a public road. The man, before alighting, asked, "Do you know a George W. Jones?" I replied, "That's my name, sir," much surprised to hear him call my name. "Well, did you ever know a fellow named Jeff Davis?" asked the man. "Why I should think I did. I went to school with him in Kentucky." "Well, I'm Jeff," was the reply. "The devil you are," Said I. "Why Jeff, blast your hide, get down and come in."

Jeff, had been from Fort Dodge to Galena hunting deserters, and hearing that I lived in the country, came by, out of ; his way, to see me. He was then a Lieutenant in the army, and as fine a looking fellow as you ever saw. There is a prevalent opinion that Jeff, had to run away with Zach Taylor's daughter to marry her. That is a mistake, as I happen to know the facts. Gen. Taylor was opposed to the match, but not for personal reasons. He said to me- "I like Davis as well as any young man I know, and I would be willing for him to marry Knox (that was the name of his daughter) if he was not in the army. No woman can have her husband in the army and be happy. I already have a son-in-law who is a surgeon in the army, and it is a continual complaint in our family that our wives are almost completely cut off from association with us." His daughter was married at the house of her uncle, in Lexington, KY., but with the consent of her father. Taylor was not, however, very cordial to Davis, until the battle of Buena Vista. Davis really won that battle, and his conduct on that occasion completely won his father-in-law over to him."

In 1884, GEN JONES' PUBLIC CAREER

began. In that year he was sent as a delegate to Congress from the Territory of Michigan. Michigan then included what is now Michigan, Wisconsin, Iowa, Nebraska and all the Northwestern country extending to the Pacific coast. The trust was an important one and General Jones was kept busy attending to the interests of his constituents. Here began an eventful career in Congress that lasted through seventeen years, five years as a Territorial delegate and twelve years a Senator from the State of Iowa. As a delegate he affiliated with neither political party, but while Senator he was always a pronounced Democrat and noted for his aggressive views on all party questions: For many years he was an intimate associate of Gray, Webster, Benton, Wise, Franklin, Pierce, and many of the other distinguished statesmen who figured at Washington during his term of service there.

SPEAKING OF WEBSTER,

Gen. Jones said: "Our country produced no more honest man, nor one of greater intellect. I had intimate business and social relations with him for many years and there were none better able to judge of him than me. Webster and myself had a land-speculating partnership in Michigan for a long time, and his profits of my transaction amounted to $75,000.

Much criticism was passed on Webster about his failure to pay debts. Webster was a poor fellow to pay debts, but this weakness did not arise from any dishonesty. It came from an inability to realize the value of money. He squandered it and threw it away without once thinking where he was to get more, or how he was to pay outstanding obligations. He died owing me $1,500, but there was never a purpose on his part to evade its payment. He thought of nothing but political ambition. He was wrapped up in that one idea, and cared little for society except that of ladies."

SECOND TO CILLEY.

Gen. Jones was a second to Cilley in his famous duel with Graves, and speaking of that historic affair he said. "I was virtually forced into that affair by Franklin Pierce. I will tell you how it was. At the time the duel occurred I was rooming at a hotel where a friend of mine, a Dr Linde, also had rooms. Linde was sick and I was in the habit of going into his room to see how he was getting on. One day I dropped in and I found in the room Benton, of Missouri, Franklin Pierce, of New Hampshire, and Dr. Duncan, of Cincinnati. When I entered, these gentlemen were conversing about something which I did not understand. Benton said: "Well, there is no way of getting out of a fight;" then there was a talk about rifles and pistols which I did not understand. After staying a few minutes I returned to my room and sat down to wait for the dinner bell to ring. Within a few minutes Pierce came and said: "See here, Jones, Cilley wants you to act as his friend."

"Friend for what"" asked I, "explain, I do not know what you mean."

"Why," replied Pierce, "haven't you heard that Graves has challenged Cilley and that Cilley has determined to accept? He wants you as first choice, and if you will not act his second choice is Governor Miller, of Missouri."

I was perfectly astounded and immediately replied. "Why, Pierce, I can't take part in such an affair. I have several important bills before Congress, and if I go out with Cilley it will destroy my influence here and ruin me with my constituents."

"But," said Pierce, "Cilley is anxious to have you, and he will be greatly disappointed if you do not act. Come into the room with Benton and Duncan, and let's have a talk."

"Well, we went to Linde's room, where Benton and Duncan were still talking about the duel. I again assured these gentlemen that I could take no part in the meeting, and Pierce again said Cilley would certainly depend on me.

99

Going to a bureau, Dr. Duncan said-"Here is the weapon Cilley will fight with." It was a short rifle of peculiar make, and did not look like a very

FORMIDABLE WEAPON.

I said, "This rifle is too small to fight with; why does not Cilley get a bigger gun?"

Dr. Duncan replied, "You are mistaken if you do not think that rifle is a dangerous weapon. I had it made for my own use, and I can pick a squirrel off a tree 200 feet high with it."

Well, Cilley sent for me to come and see him, and I went. He said to me, "Look here, Jones, you are going to stick by me, are you not?"

I replied, "Cilley, it will ruin me to act as your second, and therefore I will have to ask you to call on some other friend."

Cilley then rather importuned me to see him through. He had been to see Miller, and Miller had refused to act. I was the only person upon whom he could call. The affair would ruin him In Maine also, but there was no rescue but to fight. If he did not accept the challenge, Graves, who was a large, powerful man, would assault him in the street and cowhide him. Cilley was a very impressive talker and he so impressed me that I suddenly interrupted him and said, "That's enough, I will stand by you "

Said I, "why do you want to fight with a rifle?"

Cilley replied that he had named a rifle because he thought Graves, like most Southerners, was an expert with pistols, and not particularly so with rifles, and that with these weapons he would be on nearer terms of equality than with any other arm. He had been out practicing with a rifle, and had made several good shots. Well, to make a long story short, I acted as second to Cilley, and he was mortally wounded,

100

as everybody knows.

ELECTING DEAN CHAPLAIN.

One of the most notable things that General Jones did while in Congress, and one for which a grateful people will ever remember him, was to have Henry Clay Dean elected Chaplain of the United States Senate. "I'll tell you how that was done," said General Jones. "I was in Iowa, at the house of a clerical friend, when the question of the election of a Chaplain to the United States Senate came up. Henry Clay Dean's name happened to be mentioned in a harmonious way, and I said, by George I believe I will have friend Dean elected to the Chaplaincy." My host laughed heartily and said, "Why, you'll never get Dean to put on a clean shirt." I replied, "Oh, I'll take care of that; me and my wife will get him in Washington, and when we get through with him would not recognize the same old Dean. "I went to the Capitol and nominated Dean for Chaplain, and he was unanimously elected. We had a hard time in getting Dean to fix him up decently, but we took him to our house, got him a new suit of clothes, and though he did not look dressed he was at least respectable in appearance. My wife had to watch him all the time. That man has the strongest aversion to a clean shirt of any human being I ever saw. He had to be almost forced to put on fresh linen, and, though his clothes were the finest that could be bought he always looked sloven. He seemed to defy all the arts of the tailor, the barber and the washerwoman. It took my wife about half the time to look after Dean, but she succeeded, in spite of his affinity for dirt, in always sending him out in semi-respectable shape. We thought we had Dean partially reformed, but as soon as he left Washington and returned home he fell into his old habits; in fact, I believe he took on a little more soil than ever before, and ever since he has been a stranger to bath-tubs and clean shirts.

SENT TO FORT LAFAYETTE

A memorable incident in Gen. Jones' career was his incarceration at Fort Lafayette at the instance of Secretary Seward, told subsequently in his own language. The incident was brought about in the following manner. "At the close of the Congressional season of 1859, I fixed up my business affairs in Washington with a view to return home and settle down to private life. Unexpectedly President Buchannan ordered me the mission to New Granada, South America, and being urged by him to accept, I did so. When our civil war came up I was at Bogota, still acting as minister. I was a strong Union man, but did not believe in coercion. I believed that in a republic a resort to arms is never justifiable in the settlement of civil disputes, and that the only constitutional way of settling the difference was by conventions and compromises in Congress. In July, 1861, not having heard from this country in over three months, and not knowing that the war had actually begun, I wrote a letter to Jeff Davis, in which I said" Dear JEFF -I want to appeal to you, as an old schoolmate and friend of forty years, not to break up our Government. It is too grand a structure to be broken to pieces, and you and your friends of the South should seek some other means as a redress for your wrongs. If fight you must, fight in the Union, and I am with you for the maintenance of the constitution to the last extremity. " This letter was addressed to Jeff Davis, care of Seward, Secretary of State. I returned to the United States in December, 1861, and went straight to Washington. I met General Shields and he asked me, "Have you seen Lincoln?" I replied that I had not, and would be glad to be introduced to him. "Come right along," said General Shields. "I am going to the Capitol, and I will present you.' We were ushered into the room, and was presented to the President. There was present Montgomery Blair, Francis P. Blair and George D. Prentice. They were there for the purpose of interceding for the release of a friend confined in Fort Lafayette. We had a very pleasant interview, in which President Lincoln reminded me that I had once met him in Illinois, and that I knew his wife, formerly Miss Todd, when she lived in Lexington, Ky. During his conversation he brought in his inevitable, "this reminds me of a little anecdote, and he did tell me several anecdotes that made us laugh heartily. The next day

SECRETARY SEWARD

gave me a dinner, inviting a number of distinguished gentlemen, and paying me special honor. At this time he still had in his possession the letter I had written to Jeff Davis, and also the letter of my wife written to her friends, though he never once mentioned the letter. In ten days, I was, much to my surprise, arrested, informed that I was charged with treasonable letters, and sent to Fort Lafayette. My friend, Gen. Shield, of Carrollton, Mo., went to see Seward and said, "Mr. Secretary, I am astonished at the proceedings against Gen. Jones. I know him to be a strong Union man as you do, and it is certainly a very great outrage to have him arrested and imprisoned on a charge that can never be sustained "

Seward laughed, and replied that he knew I was a good Union man, but my wife was a terrible rebel, that two of my sons had gone South and joined the Confederate army, and that the rebel element of Dubuque needed a severe lesson that could not be more effectually taught than by my arrest. I was confined in Fort Lafayette sixty-four days, after which I was released without trial, and permitted to go where I chose. I remained in Iowa during the remainder of the war. Shortly after being released I brought suit against Seward for $50,000 damages. The case was pending at the time of his death, and if he had not died before the trial I feel certain I would have obtained judgment for the full amount"

Death of Clark Meeker

In the Mar 31, 1887 edition of "THE KEOKUK
CONSTITUTION", tells of Clark Meeker's life and recent
death.

From a letter recently received by Mrs. Henry D. Bartlett
from a relative in California, it is learned that Aaron Clark
Meeker, once known to the remaining few early settlers of
Keokuk, died at his home at Lodi, California, and was
buried at Woodbridge, San Joaquin County, February 27th,
1887. Mr. Meeker and his wife were here on a visit two
years ago and at that time gave the writer the following
sketch of himself and some early reminiscences of Keokuk,
which may be interesting to your readers now:

"I was born in Millersburg, Schoharie County, New York,
August 16th, 1813. Two years after my birth, my father,
Ephraim Meeker, moved to Ohio, and settled at
Millersburg, Cuyahoga County, and was a common
laborer. I was the oldest child of my parents. When I was 9
years of age, my father moved back to New York state and
lived six years at Coxsackie, on the Hudson River. During
this time I ran away from home, went to sea on a merchant
vessel from New York City and made a trip to Liverpool,
England. My father notified the police of New York, and
on the return of the vessel I was arrested and sent home.
My father then moved back to Millersburg, Ohio, and in
the spring of 1837, to Chillicothe. I received no education
except the early instruction my mother could give, and the
occasional pedagogue at the log school house. I learned
something from the few books at home, reading at night by
the light of a tallow candle, which I helped "dip" from the
tallow of a deer killed by my father in the neighborhood.
At 17 years of age I went to Strongville and served 3 years
at the carpenter's trade with Ebenezer Pomroy. On

February 17th, 1836, I was married to Lydia Gardner at Millersburg, Ohio, we having known each other from childhood. I engaged in business as an undertaker at Chillicothe until 1840, when, with my father's family, and in company of Dr. Isaac Galland and others, we moved to Keokuk, Iowa territory. We landed at Keokuk on May 5th, 1840. At that time there were about seven log cabins and the leading citizens were Mrs. Gaines, Wm. McBride, Henry J. Campbell, Paul DuShaun (Paul Bressett) , Louisa Hood, Ed. Brishnell, Val VanOrsdall and others. When I landed my family, consisting of myself, wife and two children, father, mother and three sisters, the only accommodation we could get, was a log cabin, 10x12 feet, near the foot of Main street, owned by Mrs. Gaines, used as a turkey roost, and it was a constant fight between us and the turkeys as to which should occupy the cabin for the first night. We paid $3 per month rent. The first work I got was on the old Keokuk house, then being built on the levee, between Main and Johnson streets.

"My father, mother and sisters were all taken sick, and I secured a place for them at Joe Robert's place about three miles above town, near the mouth of Price's Creek. My wife walked there every day to see and take care of them; while I was working to keep them all in provisions and medicines. This first summer we were unfortunate in the loss by death of both of our children, one dying on the 8th and the other on the 9th of July, and were buried in the same grave on the farm of Wright & Touse, afterwards owned by Breckenridge. Sammy Wright and Major Touse. were two Englishmen, bachelors, living together on their farm, which included what is now Kilbourne's addition, the farm house standing near where is now the corner of Sixteenth and Des Moines streets. No other children were born to us, and we are now bordering on fifty years of married life, childless.

"After the death of our children, I went to work to build me a house. There being no mill or lumber here, I went up the

106

river towards Nashville, cut logs, rafted them to Warsaw, had them sawed by old man Chittenden, who had a saw mill there, loaded the lumber on a keel boat and towed it up by hand to Keokuk. I built a house on the southeast side of First street, between Main and Johnson, size 16x24 feet. This was the first frame dwelling built in the town. Before it was completed I rented it for $8 per month, and set up some boards on the corner of First and Johnson streets, where myself and wife remained until I built a frame house on lot 9, block 3. The next year I built the brick building now standing on the same lot, and opened it as a hotel, calling it the American House, using the frame addition as a dining room and kitchen. This was the second brick house built in Keokuk, the first one having been erected by Lyman E. Johnson on the southeast corner of Main and Second streets, then considered in the country, and afterwards sold to and occupied by Uncle Johnny Graham as a residence. (This building is now being razed to allow the Irwin-Phillips Company to erect their fine business block.) The third brick house built in Keokuk was that now standing on lot 3, block 5, built by Chittenden & McGavic in 1846. The fourth brick house was built by "Citizen" A. Brown on lot 5, block 6, and built partly in Water street,

"About 1840, Orin Webb and Geo. Knight became possessed of a grizzly bear from the Rocky Mountains and kept it about 3 years, until it weighed about 1,000 pounds. In the summer of 1843, a circus and menagerie came to town and the men stopped at my house. They had two large Santa Fe bears[133] and while here purchased the grizzly from Webb and Knight, paying $40 for it, and being unable to take all three with them, on their departure made me a present of one of the Santa Fe bears, I giving them $3 for the cage in which it was kept. The keeper of the bear chained him up to my sign post in front of the hotel and the cage was placed in the back yard. The bear was kept chained in front of the hotel for a month or two. The circus

---

[133] Bears from Santa Fe, NM

men put the grizzly in the same cage with the Santa Fe and started by wagon to La Grange, Mo. , where they gave their next exhibition. The cage was closed, and upon arriving at La Grange, and opening it, they found only the grizzly inside with the bones of the other. During the time my bear was chained to the sign post, I went off on a hunt in, Missouri, and while gone, a carpenter named Thurman, "Old Chips," as he was called, got on a spree, taking a bundle of coon skins under his arm, went from house to house trying to sell them. Finally he came around to where the bear was chained and began teasing him, when the bear made one grab for him taking out the seat of his pantaloons. Thurman then swore vengeance against his bearship, and fearing trouble, I put him in his cage, intending later to serve him up on my table. I left home again for another, hunt and during my absence, Thurman, Capt. Bill Holliday, "Bucket" Campbell and Bill Clark concluded to have some fun by releasing the bear. Holiday kept some hounds, and they expected the bear to take to the woods, and have a nice chase. They went to work with an auger and bored out a place large enough for the bear to escape. As soon, as released the bear went to the kitchen window, putting his paws against it, broke it in with a crash and aroused the neighborhood. A crowd soon gathered with rifles and shot guns, shooting the poor bear to death in the yard, thus spoiling the fun of the party who was anticipating an exciting bear chase.

"In 1848-9 the discovery of gold in California induced a large emigration to the Pacific coast. I caught the fever, and on the 3rd day of December, 1849, in company with Ross B. Hughes, __Fulsom, Z.P. Meeker, W.F. Meeker, John Billings and others, left Keokuk, by steamboat for New Orleans, thence by way of Panama to San Francisco. We were detained on the isthmus[134] about 6 weeks and

---

[134] a narrow strip of land with sea on either side, forming a link between two larger areas of land; in this case Panama, about 50 miles overland. (No canal existed until 1914.)

arrived at San Francisco March 1st, 1850. I went direct to Sacramento and there found work at my trade as carpenter at twenty dollars per day. After four weeks work I went to the mines at Auburn and thence to Eldorado, where I met Dr. Todd, an old settler on the Des Moines River, who was keeping a ranch and boarding house. He charged us four dollars per meal, and on account of old acquaintance and the respect he had for my family he offered to sell me beef at one dollar and a half per pound. Having been a good rifle shot and hunter all my life, I took my gun and went out a short distance, killed two deer, brought them in and my old friend, the doctor, would only offer me 75c. per pound for the meat. I took possession of a stump near by, using it for a meat block, cut up my venison and sold it out to the miners at one dollar per pound. After mining some time, in the fall of 1850, I came to Sacramento with the intention of returning to Iowa. There I found "Old Split Log" Mitchell and his family. The cholera broke out about that time and I concluded to stay on land rather than take my chances on board a crowded ship. I took up my home with "Old Split Log." While there Mitchell was taken with cholera and died. I then went to Feather River,, where I was elected alcalde[135] or justice of the peace. I returned to Iowa by way of Panama and New Orleans, arriving at Keokuk in the winter of 1852. In April, 1853, I left my Iowa home again for California, this time going overland by ox team, with my wife, father, mother, and brother Wesley. In our train[136] were also Val Vanorsdall, his sister, Mrs. Stillwell, Lizzie Stillwell, her niece and daughter of Louisa Hood; W.F. Meeker, wife and children, Bird and wife, a man named Braffet and a blacksmith who worked for Charlie Moore. We were six months on the road, arriving at Placerville, in October, 1853. From there I went to Elkhorn township, San Joaquin County, and have lived

---

[135] (in Spain and Spanish America) the mayor or chief magistrate in a town.
[136] Wagon train as the Transcontinental Railroad was not completed until 1869.

there ever since. In 1865, I was elected justice of the peace, and commenced the Study of law which I continued during my nine years service in that position. I am now engaged in the practice of law and real estate business at Lodi, San Joaquin County, and at this date, June 16th, 1884, am back to my old Keokuk home on a visit with my wife, enjoying for a few days the company of such of our old friends as still remain here, before going back to our California home, where we have accumulated enough of this world's goods to enable us to spend the remainder of our days there in comfort and happiness."

An incident of early times in which Meeker was a prominent actor is related by an old settler. In May 1849, a strange woman came to Keokuk and stopped at the house of "Citizen" Brown. He was called "Citizen," to distinguish him from another, Andy Brown. No one knew whence the woman came, but it was soon discovered that she was mentally deficient or partially insane, and there being at that time no suitable place (poor house) for the care of such persons, she became a great burden, and the city authorities were appealed to make some disposition of her. Upon consultation it was decided to put her on a steamboat and send her to Rock Island. It was necessary, however, to send some discreet[137] person to accompany her and so place her in Rock Island that the manner of her arrival and where from should not be known. Clark Meeker was the man selected for this delicate duty. All expenses and his per diem[138] was to be paid from the city treasury. Some instructions were being given him as to the best mode of accomplishing the object of his trip when Meeker remarked that their advice and instructions were entirely gratuitous and unnecessary, saying: "I have been to mill three times and to church once and I know a thing or two, and I think myself amply qualified to manage a little thing like this."

---

[137] careful and circumspect in one's speech or actions, especially in order to avoid causing offense or to gain an advantage.
[138] Per day in Latin.

110

Meeker started with his charge and on the arrival of the boat at Rock Island found a place to "put up," and leave the woman. To throw the people off his track it was his intention to proceed on up the river, but before the boat left the landing the attempted injustice to Rock Island became known and Meeker was arrested. Without any legal ceremony, they took him and the woman, placed them both in an old queensware crate[139], fastened down the top, placed the crate on a two-wheeled cart, drove around town on exhibition, then to the wharf where there was another boat going down the river, placed the crate on board and had it regularly billed for Keokuk, where in due time they arrived in safety. The woman was then placed with a family here to be cared for, and soon after died of cholera. Meeker was ever after reminded of his experience in going to mill and church. At that time our city council consisted of six alderman, presided over by Mayor , Uriah Raplee. There is but one member of that council living to day, A.B. Chittenden, Esq., who has been a continuous resident of the city since 1840.

---

[139] Queensware (inexpensive cream china from England) was shipped from England to America, up the Mississippi in large wooden crates.

J C Parrott - Sixty Two Years

In the Dec 23, 1896 edition of "CONSTITUTION-DEMOCRAT", Col. J.C. Parrott tells of his life on the Iowa Frontier.

Col. J. C. Parrot

Col. J.C. Parrott Has Lived in Iowa That Long - "Writes of Early Reminiscences.

Sunday's Des Moines Leader contained a series of articles by some of the pioneers of Iowa, together with the portraits of a group of these pioneers. Col. J.C. Parrott of this city was one of the contributors and his portrait appears with the others. Col. Parrott says in a letter to the Leader: "My article is written entirely from memory, having no notes at hand for reference. I am old and feeble and still enjoy life with my good wife of over fifty-eight years of married life."

Col. Parrott's article is as follows:

I came to what is now Lee County, Iowa, on the 27th day of September, 1834. I was first sergeant of Co. I, First United States Dragoons at that time, which with companies B and H formed a detachment of said regiment to occupy Camp Des Moines, which garrison was located at the head

113

of the Des Moines Rapids of the Mississippi where the town of Montrose is now situated.

Co. I was commanded by J.B. Browne, Captain Abraham Van Buren, first lieutenant; A.M. Lea, second lieutenant; and A.G. Edwards[140], brevet second lieutenant. Co. B was commanded by Capt. E.V. Summer, H.C. Turner, first lieutenant. Co. H was commanded by Nathan Boone, Capt. B.B. Roberts, second lieutenant. Capt. Boone was a son of Daniel Boone of Kentucky, and was a "chip off the old block."

Lieutenant Colonel S.W. Kearney was in command of the detachment, B.F. Roberts's adjutant and quarter master.

The regiment was commanded by Henry Dodge, Colonel S.W. Kearney, lieutenant colonel, and R.B. Mason, major. At its organization Jefferson Davis of southern fame was its adjutant.

In 1835 Robert E. Lee, of the engineer corps, U.S.A., was assigned to duty on the Des Moines Rapids, and I made many details[141] for him of men to row his boats and set his buoys. While engaged at that time Lieut. Lee was a young man, handsome as a woman and one of the most perfect gentlemen I ever met.

When the detachment arrived Lieutenant Crossman, quarter-master, U.S.A., was erecting quarters which were completed about November 1 and occupied by troops until January, 1837. During said occupancy the detachment made campaigns in 1835-'36 through what is now the states of Iowa and Minnesota.

In the spring of 1835 we started from Camp Des Moines, proceeded north as far up as the foot of Lake Pepin. From

---

[140] Was set as Edwads in error, Albert Gallatin Edwards was the Brevet Second Lieutenant of the First Dragoons and also founder of A.G. Edwards Investments b. 10/15/1812 d.4/30/1892.

[141] a small detachment of troops or police officers given a special duty.

there we dropped down to Wabash Prairie[142], where we remained in camp for about four weeks. From there to the headquarters of the Des Moines River, thence down said river to the present cite[143] of your city. We camped on the East Side opposite the mouth of Coon River, where was made a large canoe, which in command of A.M. Lea, topographical engineer, proceeded down the river to its mouth, hunting a location for garrison, when your city was selected for that purpose.

In 1836 our campaign was through, Illinois to Chicago, thence to Milwaukee and Green Bay, returning by way of Prairie du Chien down through Galena, Rock Island, Ill., to Fort Madison, where we ferried the river, thence to Camp Des Moines, where we remained during the winter.

During the years 1835-36-37 there were many Indians around the garrison. Of the Sac and Fox tribes, Keokuk and Black Hawk of the Sacs, and Wapello and Appanoose of the Fox tribes were regular visitors to the garrison.

I was discharged February 10, 1837, and located at Fort Madison, where I remained until 1852, when I came to Keokuk, where I am still living.

I was married in Fort Madison in September, 1838. We had eight children born to us, five of whom are still living. My wife is still with me. I am old and feeble now, approaching my 86th year, but still enjoy life.

In June, 1837, Camp Des Moines was vacated and the troops went to your location and built what was known as Fort Des Moines. J.C. Parrott,

Late colonel Seventh Iowa infantry.

Keokuk, Iowa, December 14.

---

[142] Prairie near Montrose, IA

[143] Misspelling of site or location

115

A Lee County Pioneer- J.W. Campbell

In the Nov 18, 1897 edition of "", Capt. J.W. Campbell tells of early times in Iowa Territory.

Captain 'J.W. Campbell of Fort Madison Talks Interestingly of Early Times.

Des Moines Capital: If a visitor of Fort Madison is fortunate enough, to have as guide Capt. J.W. Campbell, much may be learned about the old fort. He will show where the line of sawn oak pickets that formed the 12-foot stockade, began and ended; will locate the old parade ground, and the spot, a little farther up the bend of the river, where the block house was placed as a protection against covert attacks from the Indians at this particularly exposed point. He will hand you a drink from the first well ever dug on Iowa soil, the one made by the soldiers in 1808, which has been carefully preserved through his efforts. So thoroughly and exhaustively has Capt. Campbell studied the site and construction of the old fort that he has recently drawn, in Collaboration with Mr. W.I. Morrison, a "Conceptional Bird's-eye View of Old Fort Madison." This will be further elaborated and probably painted in oils by his gifted wife, thus preserving an exact and accurate reproduction of the ground plan of the first fort built on Iowa soil. Capt. Campbell has himself had an interesting history, and although the facts have been recorded by his own facile pen in the 'History of Lee County" and in many newspaper articles, it is interesting to sit with him before a bright wood fire (the handsome brass andirons, by the way, once belonged to the Mormon prophet, Joseph Smith) on a chilly November afternoon and hear the story from his own lips.

His grandfather, Capt. James White, once owned the land where now stands the town of Nauvoo, Ill., having bought it of a French trader, Julien, in 1825. He built, in 1828, the

117

old stone mansion which is still preserved standing high up on the bluff at Nauvoo. The visitor in these parts may stop at Montrose, take the ferry boat that plies across the river and spend a pleasant half hour exploring this historic building for himself. Capt. White was a genial, jovial man, keeping "open house" the year round his decanters on the sideboard always filled with the best of whiskey, with a barrel in reserve against need.

Once a stranger, evidently well-to-do, dressed in finest broadcloth and carrying an ivory headed cane, after a night's entertainment, made the great mistake of asking for his bill. The captain's wrath rose at once. "By the eternal God," he said, "I want you to know we make no charges." During the Black Hawk war this building was a refuge for the people for fifty miles around. It has, at one time and another sheltered many famous people, the Indian chiefs Wapello and Black Hawk, General Scott, General Henry Dodge, Zackary Taylor, Abraham Lincoln, Robert E. Lee, Jefferson Davis, Daniel F. Miller and Will Carleton the poet. Joseph Smith also "had many a revelation within its walls." The first court held in Hancock County, Ill. , was held in this same house October, 1829. Capt. White eventually sold it to Isaac Galland, and he in turn to Sidney Rigdon, chief apostle of the Latter Day Saints, who moved into it in 1839. A fine oil painting of the old house, executed by his wife, now hangs in Capt. Campbell's home.

Capt. Campbell's father, I.R. Campbell, established a trading house in what is now Keokuk as early as 1831. He was a very handsome man. A large picture frame in his son's house contains his photograph, together with eight of his associates and friends-Capt. Wm. Phelps, Capt. D.S. Harris, Capt. James May, H.L. Dousman, Antoine Le Claire, Brisboe, Black Hawk and Keokuk. Most of the white men named were, like himself, river men and Indian traders. Isaac Campbell was a close friend of Black Hawk and the last time that brave old Indian was at Fort Madison, July 4, 1838, he went with him to view the place, where with his braves in 1812 he tried to fire the old fort. Soon after that Black Hawk was taken ill. Mr. Campbell visited him a few days before he died, and was presented as a dying gift from the old chief, with a handsome buckskin purse.

Capt. Campbell himself was born about forty miles below what is now Keokuk. Black Hawk's wigwam was but 100 yards from his father's house and it is no wonder that when a boy he could speak the Indian language as readily as the English. He received his early education in the first school house ever built in Iowa, with Berryman Jennings, the pioneer school teacher, as his instructor. Later he had as teacher Hon. Wm. Patterson, who was about that time writing his Life of Black Hawk. In 1844 the captain began his river life as cook in a keel boat, the "Des Moines Belle," which ran between the mouth of the Des Moines River and the Raccoon Forks. At that time only a military post existed on the site of the city of Des Moines and the Indians often hailed the boat from the shore, "Give us whisky-fire water." In 1848 the captain witnessed the burning of the old Mormon temple. He has many interesting relics, and shows with pride a flint lock gun given by Black Hawk to his father in 1834, "the first gun I ever shot after I was through with the bow and arrow."

Capt. Campbell has always realized the importance of preserving early Iowa history, and the fact that he has done what he could for his part of the state in this direction is attested by his scrap books which have been in much demand and have traveled many hundred miles to aid in historical research. The character of his collections may be shown by the following titles gleaned in turning over the pages, "Nauvoo Mormon Temple," "Up the Mississippi," "Pioneer Reminiscences," "First Side Wheeler Built in Iowa," "Iowa District of Wisconsin T'y[144].," "Iowa's First Fort," "Memories of Black Hawk," "Montrose History,"

---

[144] Abbreviation for Territory

"Wit and Wisdom of Chief Keokuk," "Exodus of Iowa Tribes," "Territorial Days in Iowa," etc., etc.

Although it is 67 years since Capt. Campbell first stepped foot on Iowa soil he is an erect, vigorous man, and can boast of but few gray hairs. He is, as has been said, "doubtless the best posted man now living on the history of the Upper Mississippi."

Alexander Cruikshank

In the Dec 27, 1878 edition of the "KEOKUK CONSTITUTION", The life of Alexander Cruikshank is provided by an Old Settler.

Alexander Cruikshank was born in Norway in 1805. Moved from Schuyler County Illinois to Lee County in the spring of 1834. At "The Point" (now Keokuk) he hired a canoe into which he placed his little traps[145] and making a sail out of his blanket he paddled and sailed to Fort Madison. The water was rough and several times he thought he and canoe would part company. When he reached Fort Madison there were but three settlers at the place, Peter Williams, Nathaniel Knapp and Richard Chaney. Mr. Cruikshank did not remain long but started out intending to seek a location on the Skunk River. He located about two miles southeast of (now) Lowell and about the same distance from Skunk River, on which he broke about eleven acres and put in a crop of sod corn.

The summer of 1834 he spent partly on his claim and partly at Fort Des Moines (Montrose), where he assisted in the building of the barracks. He burnt lime and built stone chimneys. He sold out his first claim in the fall of 1834 and took another near what is now Clay Grove, now occupied by Berry Wilcoxen, where he wintered in 1834-35 alone in his cabin. He saw but few whites this winter. At one time, for six weeks he did not see a white face. The farm of widow Price in Pleasant Ridge township now covers part of Mr. C's first claim. When Mr. C. first settled there were no settlers west of Ft. Madison.

In the summer of 1835 he broke about 20 acres of his second claim and put in a crop of sod corn.

---

[145] personal belongings; baggage.

In the fall of 1835 Stephen Perkins, Mr. C.'s father-in-law, came to him bringing his wife, whom he had left in Illinois. Edley McVey and Miles Driscoll had located a short time previously near what is now Dover. George Perkins, a brother of Mrs. C. also came in the fall. In the fall of 1835 Mr. C. sold his second claim to a Mr. Davis, of Illinois, but he never came to it, and in turn sold, to John Martin, who moved onto it in the spring of 1836.

Stephen Perkins located what is now the farm of Arch. Courtright, near Clay Grove, Samuel Paschal, who also came with Perkins, located a mile and a quarter east of Clay Grove.

McVey and Driscoll, above mentioned, were brothers-in-law, and came from Southern Illinois. They both moved to Jefferson County afterwards, where McVey died, and where Driscoll was still living at last accounts. Cruikshank located a third claim, where he still lives.

A Mr. Whitaker made a claim in 1834 where West Point now is, but never occupied it; sold the next year to a man named Howell from Illinois. Whitaker was a young man of fine education and a good surveyor, but of a roving disposition; had been to Texas previous to the rebellion against Mexico.

Mr. Hunter, a blacksmith, made a claim; in the fall of 1834, near and northeast of West Point, where Anthony Stoddard now lives. Hunter was from Tennessee, and was the first blacksmith in what is now Lee County. He got coal near the present farm of Alex. Cruikshank, where it cropped out of the bank.

Zedekiah Cleveland settled about two miles west of West Point in 1835. He was from, Washington County, New York.

Lewis Pitman settled the same year, east of West Point.

In 1836, those settling in the near neighborhood of Mr. Cruikshank, were Elias and James Overton, Solomon

Jackson, Luke Alphin and Joseph Carmack, and about West Point were James Scott, Grant, Whitehead and Levi Jackson, with their families, also David Driscoll, father of Miles. He died in 1838.

The township lines in the neighborhood of Mr. C., were run in the spring of 1836 by Capt. Parks, of Michigan, who had been a government surveyor for 20 years. The section lines were run the same year by a surveyor from Indiana.

The very first settlers lived on game and parched corn and wore leather breeches. In 1835 there were no mills in the vicinity. In the fall of that year Nathaniel Knapp put a horse mill for grinding corn at Ft. Madison. A mill on Fox River, near Waterloo, Missouri, was sometimes visited in 1835 and '36. In 1835 Mr. C. went to Rall's mill, in Schuyler County, Illinois.

In the fall of 1835 Mr. Moffatt began the erection of his mill, at Augusta, but it was not ready for business until 1836. Moffatt did a splendid business when it was finished. Mr. C. has been there a week at a time awaiting his turn. Moffatt took toll, outrageously, too. Before emptying the corn from a sack he made a mark indicating the top of the corn. He returned meal poured in lightly until the mark was reached, and if the owner gave it a shake to "settle it," it was poured out and filled up loosely again.

A horse mill for corn grinding was in operation at what is now Lowell in 1836.

The first cabins of the settlers were of round logs - sometimes "scalped" on the inside, and chinked with wood and mud mortar.

Indians were plenty in those early days. Mrs. Cruikshank cooked meals at least twice for Black Hawk, he tending her baby James (born in 1835) while she prepared his food.

Black Hawk's last visit was about six weeks before his death. He wore a plug hat, high top boots and leggins, and (shall we say it) was very drunk.

The Indians were inordinately fond of red pepper, and when any of them were about the cabin, it was necessary to hide it or it would be begged away.

The first sermon preached in Cruikshank's neighborhood was at the house of George Perkins on Sugar Creek in the spring of 1836. John Martin, a Baptist, was the preacher.

The first school was taught in a house built on the claim of George Taylor, by a Mr. Turner from North Carolina in the summer of 1839. The first school house in Franklin township was built of logs on the western boundary of Mr. Cruikshank's farm in the winter of 1839. Mr. Turner taught the first school in the new house.

In the days of the first settlers game was abundant. Deer in droves of 20 or 30 were not uncommon sights. Turkeys were not very plenty, but prairie chickens[146] were innumerable. Bears were never seen. Mr. C. knows of but one ever being killed in this country. Bees and wild honey abundant. Quails and rabbits made their appearance as the country became settled. There were plenty of wolves that committed sad havoc with the pigs and chickens. The wives of old settlers say it was nothing unusual to hear them smelling about the cabin door at night and lapping milk from the slop buckets.

The crops of the first settlers were confined to corn, pumpkins, turnips, &c.

They had great difficulty in keeping their hogs about home[147]. Many of them ran away toward the Mississippi and were killed in the bottoms. Sometimes they swam over to the islands and, it is supposed, crossed to Illinois, seeking their, old homes.

---

[146] once a very abundant bird on the prairie is now primarily limited to prairie areas in Kansas, Nebraska and South Dakota, small reconstructed prairie and brood at Kellerton, IA

[147] That is "at home" or on the farm

124

The amusements of the early settlers were shooting matches, horse races, and, when the feminine element became abundant, puncheon floor dances were held. The men often spent Sundays in hunting bee trees.

Disputes were settled by arbitration. The first Justice of the Peace in this part of the country was Edley McVey, appointed in 1836, but he never did any business.

The first marriage was Zedekiah Cleveland and Miss Anna Ware, in the winter of 1836. The bride was daughter of Lindsay Ware, who came from Illinois a few months previous and settled near Clay Grove. At last accounts Cleveland's wife was living in Davis County, Iowa, near the Missouri line.

The first birth was James Cruikshank, May 7th, 1835. The parents at that time were living on the second claim located by Mr. C., in a cabin where the Clay Grove burying ground is now located.

The first death was Mrs. Ware, mother of Z. Cleveland's wife, in August, 1838. She was buried on her husband's farm near Clay Grove, and 30 years afterward her remains were removed to another ground. The pine coffin was perfectly sound, except a small spot on the lid.

The first store in Ft. Madison was kept by Walsh & Piso, in the fall of 1834. In the winter of 1834-5 they moved to what is now Lowell or vicinity, where a camp of Indians spent the winter - but returned to Ft. Madison in the spring of 1835. Walsh & Piso came from Maryland and returned there after selling out their store. John Carroll Walsh, now a distinguished citizen of Maryland, is a member of the state senate.

Serious Accident to Keokuk

In THE DAILY GATE CITY on Nov 7, 1869, A.W. Harlan tells about a near fatal attack on Keokuk..

Some time in the month of March, 1836, Keokuk, with several lodges of his tribe, was encamped on the half-breed tract within a mile of Sweet Home, engaged in the pleasant occupation of making she-se-pac[148], (or sugar) and having a good time generally.

But Indians, like white people, sometimes get too much of a good thing. One Indian who had imbibed rather freely of the "Scoobapo" whisky, from some imaginary insult from Keokuk, resolved to kill him at once, and with a butcher knife in hand and with little ceremony, approached old K. as we called him, and at one stroke with his knife made quite a large opening into his intestines. Now here was a dilemma. The chief was stabbed, perhaps killed by an Indian; the confusion that ensued for a few minutes may be imagined.

CAPTAIN WILLIAM PHELPS.
"Che-che-pin-e-quah."

A runner was sent for his best friend, Bill Phelps; he came, saw the situation and comprehended several sides to the question at once. He put

---

[148] She-se-pac is Indian for Maple Sugar.

127

one of his hired men on a horse and started him to Ft. Madison for a Doctor; that horse made good time. The Doctor was away from home, but a youth had registered himself M.D. at a hotel; he went, dressed the wound, pronounced it dangerous but not fatal. He took up his lodging in Keokuk's (Wiekiup) lodge, stayed by him night and day, and as corn planting time approached, he got into a canoe and went with the old chief to his village near Iowaville where Phelps paid him off and he left.

I happened at Keokuk's lodge one day and enquired what boy that was living with old K. and was told that it was the Doctor. I looked at him, thought him a smart boy, but rather young to leave his mother.

A little more than fourteen years from that time I met this same boy in Sacramento City, California; he was then one of the City Council, an active member of the Board, and one of the Doctors that did not run at the approach of the terrible scourge of cholera in the fall of 1850.

We renewed our acquaintance in the Sacramento burying ground, where many of our dead friends had made their pile, though it was but a pile of sand and a wooden head board that showed where they had found a resting place. We met frequently afterwards, and he often spoke of his first case or first patient, the old Indian chief Keokuk, on the banks of that beautiful river, meaning the Des Moines.

He did not forget to inquire after his first patient or first patron, Bill Phelps. Said he, Phelps paid me well.

There was no attempt made to punish the Indian that did the stabbing; the Indian laid the crime upon the whisky. At that time I thought it an error in Indian judgment, but have long since concurred with the Indian.

Black Hawk Dancing

From the NEW-YORK AMERICAN issue dated NOV 9, 1837.

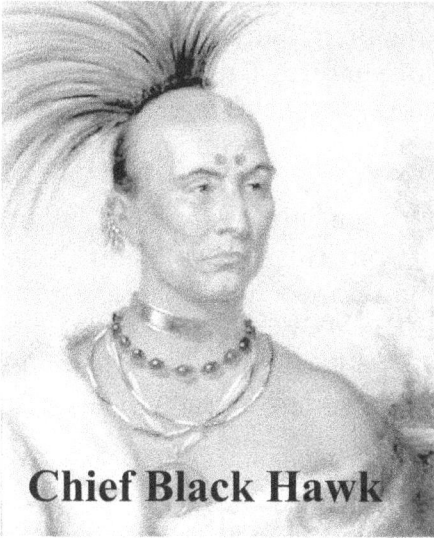

Chief Black Hawk

Young Black Hawk said he had no objection to the ladies looking at him, if they wouldn't handle him so much.- [Boston Post]

The ladies - bless their innocent hearts! - have upon all occasions evinced a just appreciation of this liberality. While in Washington, attending the councils of our red brethren, many a time and oft were we jostled from our place by some fair form more anxious than ourselves to study the 'beauties of nature.' Had our friend Mrs. Trollope been present, she might have imagined herself in the studio of some master genius, who had accomplished the miracle of producing animated statuary! An esteemed brother of the press, and a pillar of the church, too, who accompanied us to witness a war dance in one of the public squares, thus describes the scene in a letter to the Charleston Examiner:

"The party in attendance was a large one - not less than 6000 or 7000 persons being present. The spacious hall, built 6000 years ago, was lighted up as splendidly as usual, by the magnificent luminary that needs not to be replenished with oil. The Indians appeared principally in their natural covering, with the addition only of a covering of paint, and a few feathers in their hair, and rings upon their arms. The admirers of nature had therefore an excellent opportunity of studying the beauties of the human form to the best possible advantage. Some hundreds, perhaps thousands, of genteel and delicate ladies, whose excessive modesty would lead them almost to faint at the sight of a naked foot, stood it out to "the last jump." No putting up of fans, no peeping through the fingers, but stared it out with a bold face. Well-Well, if they did not blush, why should I? 'O for the good old days of Adam and Eve.' so the song goes, and today we had a touch of them."

"What was wanting in confusion, the boys happily remedied by very good imitations. So take it all in all, we ne'er may look upon its like again. The ladies declared on their way home, there was something worth seeing. A very edifying and interesting spectacle, abating the fact that some three or four who did not dance - wore blankets; this was the only drawback upon the amusements of the occasion."

The Half Breed Tract

In 1879, the Western Historical Company of Chicago printed the History of Lee County, Iowa.

Before any permanent settlement had been made in the Territory of Iowa, white adventurers, trappers and traders, many of whom were scattered along the Mississippi and its tributaries, as agents and employees of the American Fur Company, intermarried with the females of the Sac and Fox Indians, producing a race of half-breeds, whose number was never definitely ascertained. There were some respectable and excellent people among them, children of men of some refinement and education. For instance: Dr. Muir, a gentleman educated at Edinburgh, Scotland, a surgeon in the United States Army, stationed at a military post located on the present site of Warsaw (Illinois) , married an Indian woman, and reared his family of three daughters in the city of Keokuk. Other examples might be cited, but they are probably exceptions to the general rule, and the race is now nearly or quite extinct in Iowa.

A treaty was made at Washington, August 4, 1824, between the Sacs and Foxes and the United States, by which that portion of Lee County was reserved to the half-breeds of those tribes, and which was afterward known as "The Half-Breed Tract." This reservation is the triangular piece of land, containing about 119,000 acres, lying between the Mississippi and Des Moines Rivers. It is bounded on the north by the prolongation of the northern line of Missouri. this line was intended to be a straight one, running due east, which

131

would have caused it to strike the Mississippi River at or below Montrose; but the surveyor who run it took no notice of the change in the variation of the needle as he proceeded eastward, and, in consequence, the line he run was bent, deviating more and more to the northward of a direct line as he approached the Mississippi, so that it struck that river at the lower edge of the town of Fort Madison. "This erroneous line," says Judge Mason, "has been acquiesced in as well in fixing the northern limit of the Half-Breed Tract as in determining the northern boundary line of the State of Missouri,." The line thus run included in the reservation a portion of the lower part of the city of Fort Madison, and all of the present townships of Van Buren, Charleston, Jefferson, Des Moines, Montrose and Jackson.

Under the treaty of 1824, the half-breeds had the right to occupy the soil, but could not convey it, the reversion being reserved to the United States. But on the 30th day of January, 1834, by act of Congress, this reversionary right was relinquished, and the half-breeds acquired the lands in fee simple[149]. This was no sooner done, than a horde of speculators rushed in to buy land of the half-breed owners, and, in many instances, a gun, a blanket, a pony or a few quarts of whisky was sufficient for the purchase of large estates. There was a deal of sharp practice on both sides; Indians would often claim ownership of land by virtue of being half-breeds, and had no difficulty in proving their mixed blood by the Indians, and they would then cheat the speculators by selling land to which they had no rightful title. On the other hand, speculators often claimed land in which they had no ownership. It was diamond cut diamond, until at last things became badly mixed. There were no authorized surveys, and no boundary lines to claims, and, as a natural result, numerous conflicts and quarrels ensued.

---

[149] Fee simple - a permanent and absolute tenure of an estate in land with freedom to dispose of it at will (the main type of land ownership today)

To settle these difficulties, to decide the validity of claims or sell them for the benefit of the real owners, by act of the Legislature of Wisconsin Territory, approved January 16, 1838, Edward Johnstone, Thomas S. Wilson and David Brigham were appointed Commissioners, and clothed with power to effect these objects. The act provided that these Commissioners should be paid six dollars a day each. The commission entered upon its duties and continued until the next session of the Legislature, when the act creating it was repealed, invalidating all that had been done and depriving the Commissioners of their pay. The repealing act, however, authorized the commissioners to commence action against the owners of the Half-Breed Tract, to receive pay for their services, in the District Court of Lee County. Two judgments were obtained, and on execution the whole of the tract was sold to Hugh T. Reid, the Sheriff executing the deed. Mr. Reid sold portions of it to various parties, but his own title was questioned and he became involved in litigation. Decisions in favor of Reid and those holding under him were made by both District and Supreme Courts, but in December, 1850, these decisions were finally reversed by the Supreme Court of the United States in the case of Joseph Webster, plaintiff in error, vs. Hugh T. Reid, and the judgment titles failed. About nine years before the "judgment titles" were finally abrogated as above, another class of titles were brought into competition with them, and in the conflict between the two, the final decision was obtained. These were the titles based on the "decree of partition" issued by the United States District Court for the Territory of Iowa, on the 8th of May, 1841, and certified to by the Clerk on the 2d day of June of that year. Edward Johnstone and Hugh T. Reid, then law partners at Fort Madison, filed the petition for the decree in behalf of the St. Louis claimants of half-breed lands. Francis S. Key, author of the Star Spangled Banner, who was then attorney for the New York Land Company, which held heavy interests in these lands, took a leading part in the measure, and drew up the document in which it was

133

presented to the court. Judge Charles Mason, of Burlington, presided. The plan of partition divided the tract into one hundred and one shares and arranged that each claimant should draw his proportion by lot, and should abide the result, whatever it might be. The arrangement was entered into, the lots drawn, and the plat of the same filed in the Recorder's office, October 6, 1841. Upon this basis the titles to land in the half-Breed Tract are now held.

On page 531 of the same book, it tells pretty much the same thing, just going into the legal and financial aspects a little more. The only additional that might help you is this:

"A Member of the Bar" prepared a very full and concise history of the legal contest, and the status of the titles as they existed at the time, which was published in the Keokuk "Register" in December, 1848, where it is preserved, and where it may be reviewed if any of the points involved ever become subjects of controversy or dispute.

THE HALF BREED TRACT Conspiracy

In the Mar 16, 1879 edition of "The Gate City", a letter from Colonel. Albert Miller Lea tells of early times in Iowa Territory, the Iowa/Missouri border and the Half Breed Tract. After graduating from West Point in 1831, Col. Lea reported to Fort Des Moines as an engineer and was part of an expedition up the Des Moines River with Lt. Col. Kearny, Capt. Nathaniel Boone and Lt. Turner. He served as ordnance[150] officer and topographer[151], keeping track of daily travel and rate of march and sketched the route and lakes. His duties took him from the Great Lakes to the Gulf of Mexica and from Oklahoma to Tennessee. He also as chief clerk for the War Department and was Secretary of War and a Professor of Mathematics at the University of East Tennessee. During the Civil War, he served in the Confederate Army as an engineer and the Texas Calvary.

Corsicana, Texas, Feb. 18, 1879.
Mr. Justice Miller, Galveston, Texas.
Dear Sir:

Yesterday I alluded to the disputed boundary between Missouri and Iowa. There is an unwritten history connected therewith that may be worth preserving. Whilst serving at Fort Des Moines (Montrose) I heard that a few persons, including the land officers at Palmyra, had united to

---

[150] a branch of the armed forces dealing with the supply and storage of weapons, ammunition, and related equipment.
[151] a person who describes the surface features of a place or region

purchase the usufruct[152] title of certain half breed Indians, to the reservation lying between the Mississippi and Des Moines Rivers, and south of the northern boundary of Missouri extended, and that they intended to Congress for the release of the fee simple title, ostensibly for the benefit of the half breeds, who were mostly in the Rocky Mountains, but really for the benefit of the secret purchasers of their interests. They especially relied on the co-operation of Senator Benton, who was then especially powerful. This little game was quietly checked by a letter from me to Judge, H.L. White, then Senator from Tennessee and Chairman of the Committee on Indian Affairs.

Meantime the conspirators, not content with the profit to be derived from the area of the tract as it had been surveyed and settled, sought greatly to enlarge its area by removing the northern boundary of Missouri further north and consequently that of the reservation. With this view they set the pride and covetousness of the Missourians to work, and stirred up a strife that, eventually led to bloodshed. Gen. Geo W. Jones, delegate in Congress, had endeavored to settle this controversy soon after its origin, by procuring the appointment of the commission on which I served in 1838. The report made by me showed that the line long recognized had been erroneously run by reason of using the same variation of the needle from the old N.W. corner, 100 miles north of the mouth of Kansas River, to the Des Moines, thus throwing it gradually southward more and more, 1 whilst the call was for a line due east;: but it was shown also that the line was 1 so run prior to the admission of Missouri' as a State, and that it was the actual boundary with which she came into the Union. Had the correction been made as desired the northern boundary of the half breed tract would have passed to the north of Burlington. The speculation promised to be magnificent.

---

[152] The right to enjoy the use and advantages of another's property short of the destruction or waste of its substance.

My report was sent to the Senate during the winter of 1838-9. The appropriation for the survey was exhausted, and it was expected that Congress would make a further appropriation, and designate which of the several lines presented should be marked as the true boundary. Late in the session I asked Senator Linn, of Missouri, why he did not call up that matter and have it settled. He pleasantly and frankly answered that if pressed it would be settled as I had indicated, and that he did not intend that such result should take place whilst he should remain in the Senate. So, the survey was dropped, and the controversy went on until it was decided by the Supreme Court of the United States, after the admission of Iowa as a State had given her a legal standing in that tribunal. Many years after I had retired to my paternal acres in Tennessee, a request came to me from Judge Charles Mason, as attorney for Iowa, for information to enable him to assert the claim of his client; and I sent such as greatly conduced to the favorable result. Very respectfully,

Your obedient servant,

A.M. Lea

Memo. - Although not conscious of having ever been guilty of a dishonorable action, yet I am not entitled to the prefix of "Hon." which you have been pleased to give me.

I was only a Lieutenant when I left the old army; and although I have a commission as Brigadier General of militia from Gov. Chambers, of Iowa, I never exercised its functions, and was only a Major in the staff of the Confederate Army, and am generally known as such in Texas, that title having been widely noted in connection with the capture of Galveston by Magruder, when I met my oldest son, who was First Lieutenant of the Harriet Lane, and was buried with Wainwright.

After that, when I was serving with General Ben at Brownsville, Magruder issued an order promoting me to Lieut. Colonel, but that was never confirmed at Richmond, although I was thence officially known as Lieut. Colonel, and have since been recognized in society as "Col. Lea," as I am now here generally known. My service in the War Department under John Tyler, when I was for six weeks Acting Secretary of War, may afford some color to the style, but it has not been generally so given. As to the title of General, I think there should be but one General Lee (or Lea), and have declined the prefix. A.M. Lea.

Corsicana, Texas, Feb. 17, 1879.

Famous Pioneers:

Additioinal information on some of the pioneers in this book:

Chief Black Hawk (Ma-ka-tai-me-she-kia-kiak) b. 1767 in IL, was the Sauk Chief in Saukenuk, IL. He was the Sauk ally with the British during the war of 1812, holding the rank of brevet Brigadier General, in charge of all Indian Allies at Green Bay and fought the against the American forces. He was insenced when he returned to find his tribal village overran by settlers and his Sacred Burial grounds plowed and bones scattered. When he retaliated, the military drove him out. Shortly the Black Hawk war ensued. He died and was "buried" on the James Jordan farm at Iowaville, IA, only to have his bones stolen by a settler doctor, and later put on display before disappearing, presumably burned in a museum fire.

Nathaniel Boone was the youngest son of Daniel Boone, Captain in 1st US Dragoons, veteran of war of 1812, delegate of Missouri constitutional convention.

John C Breckenridge was a prominent Lawyer in Burlington. He visited his mother in Kentucky in 1843, contacted influenza and remained in Kentucky. He became Vice President with James Buchanan in 1857, lost the Presidency in 1860 to Abraham Lincoln and was the Confederate secretary of War under Jefferson Davis in 1865.

Melgar Couchman was the postmaster of Sweet Home, Missouri in 1836, Sheriff of Hancock Co, Illinois 1846-49, County Judge in 1849 and Commissioner of Hancock Co, IL 1862.

Henry Dodge was a Member of both US House and Senate, govenor of Wisconsin Territory (1836-41,1845-48) US Congressman 1841-1845). His son Agustus C Dodge was Iowa

Territorial delegate (1840, 1842, 1844-1846), Iowa Senator 1848-1855, Minister of Spain until 1859.1836 Sweet Home Ledger

Albert Gallatin Edwards was the founder of A. G. Edwards investments.

James Huston Jordan b. 1806 Frankfort, KY, d.1893 Eldon, IA.
Around 1832 opened a trading post and another one near Iowaville, IA. Was a close friend of Chief Black Hawk, secured his release from the St Louis Prison and provided him shelter near Iowaville until his death in 1838.

Thomas Jefferson Jordan b. 1805 Franklin Co, KY d. Apr 20, 1850, Belknap, Davis Co. Buried in Soap Creek Mill Cemetery.

A.M. Lea was an engineer at Fort Des Moines and surveyed southern Minnesota and Northern Iowa until his resignation in 1836. He was a brigadier general in the Iowa militia and later a major in the Confederate Army. He was also Secretary of War under John Tyler.

Robert E. Lee was the US engineer stationed at Fort Des Moines to work on navigation of the Mississippi River. Without his maps, the rapids were deadly. Later he was the commander of the Confederate Army in the Civil War.

Captain Abraham Van Buren, first lieutenant of 1st Dragoon Regiment of Fort Des Moines was the eldest son of President Martin Van Buren.

Capt. James White migrated to St Charles, MO in 1818, and by 1828 he had a two story house at Venus, IL (changed to Commerce in 1834 and Later Nauvoo, IL.) In 1832, he also built a house on the West side of the Mississippi at Montrose, IA. In 1834 the military sized his land and built Fort Des Moines. He died in Nauvoo in 1836.

Sweet Home Ledger *pages (of some settlers in this book) are from the Bedell Store in Sweet Home, Missouri during the period of 1836-1837.*

NOTE: Also served as a bank between pioneers, see above.

Sweet Home was one of the first settlements of the area as a trading post, it grew and prospered and became a river port for goods. Steamboats arrived to Sweet Home by at least 1836. It was the place most immigrants from Kentucky asked for upon arrival to ports on the Mississippi. When Athens acquired a Railroad, it grew and Sweet Home declined. The Sweet Home post office moved to Athens in 1841. The town almost completely disappeared by 1856, it is now an open field, maps show a Sweet Home Township, but most historic maps do not even show the town.

William Bedell ⟶ Dr

1836 $ c

Aug	21	1 pt Why 13¢ Ma Ointment 12¢ Whya	..	38
"	29	1 Gal Why 75¢ Sept 2nd Why 37½¢	1	12
Sept	7	1 Gal Why 75¢ ¼ # Ginger 6¼	..	81
"	8	½ pt Why 13¢ 15# 1 pt Why 25¢	..	38
"	16	1 pr Boots 400¢ 5# Coffee 100¢	5	00
"	"	3# Sugar 50¢ 1 pt Why 13¢	..	63
"	17	Why 38¢ 1 pt Why 13¢ - -	..	50
"	18	2 qts Why 50¢ 20th Salt 30¢ ..	..	80
"	23	1 gall Why 75¢ 24th Why 13¢	..	88
"	25	Shoes 450¢ Tobacco 25¢ Why 13¢	4	88
"	26	2 qts Why 50¢ oct 5th Why 37½¢	..	87
Oct	9	Flannel 5 62½¢ Why 25¢ Indigo & Mather 59¢	6	46
"	14	6d nails 75¢ 4# Allum 122 Tack nails & putty 38¢	2	12
"	22	Brandy Why & flask 62¢ 23d flask & Why 39¢	1	00
"	25	Tobacco 25¢ Why 13¢ 27th Cap 100 nails 12¢ ..	1	50
"	27	Mather 19¢ Ointment 25¢ 31st Why 62½¢	1	06
"	31	Seal Coop 1,23¢ - -	1	25
Nov	4	Pd Wilson 3 12½¢ Pd for Altrey 600¢ ..	9	13
"	5	Why 75¢ 13th Comb 25¢ 17th Tobacco 25¢	1	25
"	19	Why 75 Coffee 100¢ Sugar 50¢ indigo 20¢	2	45
"	20	Why 25¢ 27th Why 75¢ tin cups 50¢	1	50
"	28	Why 25¢ Que 1st Razor 75¢ Strop 50¢ Comb 13¢	69	
Decr	3	Why 12¢ 4th Why 25¢ 10th Suspenders 25¢	63	
"	10	Brush 18¢ Why 12¢ Soap 6¢ Why 25¢	62	
"	"	Sheeting 5 21¢ 12th Sheeting 5 40¢	10	61
"	12	Why 50¢ 16th Shoes 100¢ Why & flask 50¢	2	00
"	17	Why 13¢ Why & tobacco 38¢ Bbl & Why 62¢	1	13
"	25	Why 25¢ 30th Coffee 100¢ Sugar 100¢ Why 25¢	2	63
"	30	Combs 13¢		
			15	36 44
Jany	4	Why 25¢ Smother Why 25¢ tumbler 13¢	63	
"	6	Why 38¢ Mith 25¢ 12th Why 25¢	88	
"	17	Button 25¢ 21st Coffee 20¢ tobacco 25¢	2	50
"	21	Why 13¢		
			13	84 44

216   William Bedell   Dr

1839

Jany 21 Brot forward from Page 38 67 51 67 51

" 22 Why 13/ 26th Why 38/ 27th Sugar 50/ 1 00

" 27 Why 14/ Wine 13/ 29th Knife 25/ 50

Feb 5 Brandy 13/ 7th Stew 13/ Why 12/ "___ " 38 1 88

                            69 49

" 8 Why 25/ 10th Comb 13/ Why 38/ "___ " 75

" 11 Sugar 1 18/ Coffee 100/ Why & Stew 100/ 3 17

" 15 Mer. Ointment 50 / 16th ____ Why 13/ 50

" 17 Why 13/ 24th Tobacco 25/ Inkstand 25/ 63

" 24 Why 25/ 25th Why 25/ 28th Why 13/ 88

March 1 Why 25/ 7th Sugar 100/ Buck ram 89/ 1 44

" 7 Why 25/ 16th Why 3/4/ 17th Why 25/ 88 6 25

        Settled in full C   77 74

___

March 25 to cash 69/ 30th Why 38/ 1 07

April 6 Why 75/ 8th tea 75/ shoes 100/ sundry 2 63

" 13 Why 75/ tobacco 25/ Why 37½/ 1 38

" 20 plates 75/ tumblers 75/ tea plates 37½/ 1 38

" " Shoes 162½/ Bucket 75/ plate 37½/ 2 75

" " 2 Hats 75/ salt set 25/ mug 19/ 1 19

" 22 turpentine 31/ 24th cash 175/ 2 06

" " coffee 80/ sugar 50/ shoes 175/ 3 05

" " Why 25/ 26th comb 25/ 28th Why 38/ 88

May 3 coffee 100/ sugar 50/ Why & comb 31/ 1 81

" 4 Why 50/ 6th Why 37½/ 68

" 10 Whisky 12½/ Shoes 175 Why 25 2 12

" 12 Why 25/ 24th pepper 18/ Why 50 93

" 28 Why 37/ June to tobacco 25 hat 75 1 37

June 14 Coffee 100 Why 25/ 1 25

From 14 of June untill the 20 Sept Sundry 19 43

                   Articles 44 61

to Hawling per Renfrow 5 00

to Cash and pair Shoes 7 50

                        57 11

Joseph Benning Dr

1836				
Sept 12	1 Knight hawk 50¢			„ 50
„ 15	2½ Gallons Why 187½¢	„ „	1	87
„ 25	Coffee 10¢ Sugar 50¢ Opium 13¢	„	1	63
Oct 18	fur cap 6,0¢ 23ᵈ Sugar 50¢		6	50
„ 29	Casting 3,15¢		3	15
Nov 3	Why 75¢ Coffee 100¢ apples 13¢ „		1	88
„ 13	Salt 44¢ 23ᵈ Why 75¢		1	19
Decr 1	Suspenders 19¢ 2ᵈ Strainer 25¢ „ — „		„	44
„ 13	Why 13¢ 26ᵗʰ Copper Boiler 75¢			88
„ 26	Stew 38¢ Glasses 25¢		63	$18 68
Jany 16	Dish 38¢ Mug 6¢ Bole 50¢		„	94
Febr 5	Brandy 13¢ „ —— „ —— „ —— „		13	1 06
	settled in full			$19 74

1837				
April 4	Balance on shoes 50¢ Why 12½¢		„	63
„ 19	Sugar 100¢ 23ᵈ bull 100¢		2	00
May 19	1 Set teacups 75 Glass tumblers 25		1	00
	pr lb tea 38¢ 24 May Why 25¢		„	63
May 5	Cash Loaned $7, 00		7	00
June 12	1 hatt 75¢ July ½ shirts 25		1	00
July 4	1 oz Camphire 25¢ 22 July copr			31
			12	57
			10	00
August 25	whis 75 sept the 1st pepper 12¢	Bal	2	57
Sept 5	whis 75		„	75
„ 8	Brandy 12¢ putty 13¢ window glass 50			75
			$4	95
Dec 24	To 1 Gall Whis 100 Hitchcocks a/c 25		1	25
1838 Jany 18	To Sundrys 100 Feb 26 ¾ Sundrys 38		1	38
	To Wm Biddle private a/c 64 or Beef		2	88
			10	44

51   James & Boon   Dr
1837 $ cts

Mar 3   H tobacco 25 ¢ pounas 12 ¢   37½
   10   13 38
   11   1 Bridle $2.50, 1 plough line 19¢   2 69
   25   1 qut why 25¢ June the 2 lb rears 7¢ 1 00
June 7 p lb Ginger 19¢ Nutmeggs 12¢   ..   31
        Balance on powder 25¢   ..   25
May 13 1 Bottle mustard 25¢ comb 25¢   50
        castor 25.. comb 19¢ p lb tobaco 12¢ 56
June 15 1 Vial Batemen Droops   25
        1 Ditto Panagoric   25
     25 tobaco 13 ¢ penknife 1.00   1..13
     29 pair combs 18¢ Bonnet 13, combs 12   ,, 44
        1 pair Shoes $1.62..   1 62
July 22 whis 13¢   13
                                          _____
                                          9.88

42   John Boon   Cr
1836 $ c
oct 19 1 qt why 50¢ ..   "   "   ,, 50
Nov 2   why 150¢ Hammer 75¢ Boiler 75¢ .. 3 00
   "   " nails 100¢ Barrell 75¢ 1 75
   " 16 nails 25¢ 20 lb why 100¢   2 25 $6 50
Jany 16 Coffee 100¢ Sugar 100¢ tobacco 25¢ 2 25
   "   " Camphor 25¢ Hops 38¢ Why 88¢ Shoes 138¢ 2 88
   "   " Wine 25¢ 25 lb coffee 200¢ Rosin 13¢ 2 38
   " 25 Wine 25¢ Salt 38 lb sugar 100¢ Tea 50¢ 1.75
Feb 21 Indago 20¢   20 9.46
                                          _____
                                          15.96

1837 John Boon   Dr to am
June 20 whis 38¢ whis 37¢   ,,75 ,,
     29 whis 25¢ July the 6 whis 25   50
Aug 29 why 13¢ why 25¢   38
                                          _____
                                          1 63

William Clark   Dr

		$	c
Sept 2	2 harps 12¢ 1/2 pt Why 13¢ —	"	25
5	1 gallon Why 75 ¢ 9th 203 indigo 40¢	1	15
10	1 qt Why 25¢ 1 ℔ tobacco 25¢	"	50
15	1 hat 5.00 ¢ 5 ℔ coffee 100¢	6	00
"	3 Sugar 50¢ 1 pr shoes 75 ¢ Whyn	1	34
16	1 pr coarse Boots 4.00 ¢	4	00
17	by cash 63 ¢ 1/2 pt Why 25¢ 1/2 pt brandy 12¢	1	00
18	1 grap cord 50¢ 19 ℔ Salt 5.10¢	5	60
24	indigo 40¢ Why 13¢ 25 ℔ drops 150¢	2	28
oct 4	qt why 2 59 8th coffee 80¢	1 05	8 33 91
" 20	madder 19¢ allum 12¢ whys 12¢ —		44
" 25	chord 50¢ Why 25¢ Coffee 100¢	1	75
" 26	plates 38¢ why 13¢ 2 4 ℔ Why 13¢ tobacco		75
Nov 3	Sugar 50¢ apples 50¢ 4 ℔ Buttons 13¢	1	13
" 8	teas 1.00¢ 9 ℔ why 25¢ 11 ℔ Coffee 100¢	2	75
" 11	Sugar 50¢ Why 75¢ 13 ℔ cup 100¢	2	25
" 28	Why 13¢	"	13
" 30	1 gallon Why	"	75
Dec 11	tobacco 25¢ Why 25¢ Sugar 5¢ coffee 100¢	2	00
" "	Bottle 25¢ tea 75¢ 13 ℔ Why 30 ¢	1	50
" 20	Coffee 100¢ Sugar 100¢ Bottle & why 1.12¢	3	13
" 24	Sheeting 38¢ why 13¢ 25 ℔ Why 13¢ 2 ℔ Why 25¢		88
1857 27	tacks 11 ℔	19 8	17 65
Janry 4	tobacco 25¢ 9 ℔ Steel 25¢ 9 ℔ Sugar 50¢	1	00
" 12	Sheeting 38¢ why 13¢ 14 ℔ Why 25¢		75
" 23	cambric 38¢ Buttons 25¢ Silk 6¢ Combs 25¢		94
" "	Sheeting 4.75¢ 30 ℔ Brandy 4 flask 38¢	5	13
Feby 7	Sugar 50¢ thread 12¢ calico 62 1/2 ¢	1	25
" 10	Sugar 100¢ Why 13¢ tobacco 25¢ powder 50¢	1	50
" "	chocolate 25¢ 13 ℔ Rice 50¢ tea 75¢	1	50
" 13	Sugar 38¢ augers 138¢ gimblet 25¢	2	01
" "	hammer 75¢ chizle 50¢ 16 ℔ Why 13¢	1	38
" 17	Why 13¢ cloth 13¢	25	56 88

147

26   *William Clarke*   Dr

1837

April	7	1 gl. why 25/3th tea 33¢	65
"	20	Sugar 100¢ why 14¢ tobacco 12¢	1 25
"	22	why 75¢ 25th shoes 1.75 hdchd 50	3 70
"	28	why 18¢ to cash 2.50¢	2 63
May	4	flask & why 25/9th coffee 100¢ why 2¢	1 50
"	10	1 S.H. tea 6 cup 38¢ reasons 13 why 2¢	75
	20	1 Dipper 19,, June 4th 1 cord 50 tobacc 12	82
June	19	whis 13 tin panil 6 reasons 19	1 32
	26	pepermint 13 Spice 12	25
	21	4 lt sugar 50	50
	29	whis 13 C shoes 2.00 whis 12	2 25
July	3	Sugar 150 & salts 13¢ whis 12	75
	11	alove 13¢ reasons 6¢ whis 25 coffee 100	1 82
	18	to cas 7.00 July 22 whis & wine 25	7 25
	23	Sugar 75¢ tin pan 19¢	94
		tobacco 13¢ tin funnel 25¢	38
July	8th	whis 13¢	13
			26 17
Sept	2	to paper 18¢	18
"	23	knight glass 50¢	50
Dec	17	to Draw Chains 125 C 2 Glass whis 12 C	68
	24	to 1 Gall Whis 100 C	1 37
		to Hitchcock O/c	1 00
			10 33

148

1837 ⟶ Melgar Couchman $ Dr

May 12 ink 25.. Gritter 13.. Drinks 25..   63

June 12 Drinks 25 — —   ,, 25

    powder per William   ,, 13

Sept 4 1 pair shoes per Wright 1.75   1 75

                    2 76

Dec 31 To 1 Vial Elixer paragoric 25 discount to £3.50   ,, 75

   " Hitchcock's Alk. 400   4 00   7.51

    do do 1 At 5 00 wine &c

    Candy 25 & traded C J Wales   5 75

Apr 12 1 Hatt 4. 00 June 11 whis Bar 75   4 75

June 11 1 Gall whis 75 Candy 25 wine 25   1 25 $

                    11.75

---

204   Charles Davis   Dr

1837 $ c

Jany 15 drill 25 ⅌ flannel 188 ⅌ sugar 109 ⅌   4 13

" " Coffee 400 ⅌ Bobinett 98 ⅌ thread 137   4 91

" " Cali 75 ⅌ Ribbon 55 ⅌   1 25 10 29

March 10 4 Bbl of tar   6 00 6 00

    by Joseph Carter   1 75 16 29

                   18 04

March 25 2 phials British oil 75 ⅌   ,, 75

149

1836. Nathaniel Dews   Dr

                                                              $ | cts
            From Small Ledger Page 101.   47 |14

July 16 1 qt wine 12½ 4 igh 1½ shears 100 9 --   1 |13
  .. 27 1 p suspenders 37½ 4 why 02½ |50
aug 5 1 g why 25 9 15 ½ gall why 37½ --   1 |13
  .. 13 1 ℔ powder 75 9 5 ℔ lead 31 9 2 pipes 12½ -- 1 |19   51 |12
──
aug 20 1 whiskey 37½ g ℔ salt 196 9 | 2 |34
    31 ½ ℔ tobacco 37p 9 --   ..   .. | |38
Sept 3   Cash 5.00 9 1 girth 4 why 50 9   5 |50
   ..   1 paper tacks 17 ½ 4   ..   .. |18
    9   1 pr locks 50 9 ½ why 13 9 |63
   13   12 yds lines 2 1.00 9 1 y yds silk 2.25 9 23 |25
   "   1½ yds buckram 31 9   ..   .. |31
    14   5 ℔ coffee 1.00 9   ..   ..   1 |00
    18   2 ℔ powder 100 9 5 pr ℔ lead 56 9   .. 1 |56
  .. 23 Buckram 2 9 3 Bedcords 1.50 9 --   1 |75
oct 11 5 boxes percussion caps 1.25 9 2 qts why 50 9 1 |75
  .. 13 9 qd licking 2.25 9 2 ℔ powder 100 9 6 ℔ shot 75 9 4 |00
   .. 25 Nails 100 9 why 38 9 coffee 12½ 9 feathers 6.38 9 9 |00
   .. 30 Butts 38 4 tobacco 81 ½ 4   ..   .. 1 |19
Nov 2   why 25 9 teas 1.25 9 7 ℔ why 75 9 --   2 |25
  .. 10 why 12½ 9 N ℔ plates 38 9 why 12½ 9 |63
Jan 29 to sundry articles by bill   16 |00 871 |73
  " 25 why 88 9 3 pr why coffee 2.00 9 ..   "   2 |88   2 |88
                                                      $ 74 |61

1838 to whiskey   2.25   2.25

Jonas H. Denny Dr

<table>
<tr><td>1836</td><td></td><td></td><td></td><td></td></tr>
<tr><td>July</td><td>2</td><td>from small Legger Page 39</td><td>40</td><td>63½</td></tr>
<tr><td>"</td><td>"</td><td>.. 59. ribbon 37½¢ 2 do. do 50¢ waste do 37½¢</td><td>1</td><td>25</td></tr>
<tr><td>"</td><td>"</td><td>.. flask 200¢ 2 & 1. C. powder 37½¢ ..</td><td>2</td><td>38</td></tr>
<tr><td></td><td>31</td><td>2 Sett plate 75¢ 2 dishy 101¢ 2 pitchers 150¢</td><td>3</td><td>25</td></tr>
<tr><td></td><td>"</td><td>4 bowls 50¢ 2 wood buckets 125¢ 1 B. box 2</td><td>13</td><td>49.64</td></tr>
<tr><td></td><td></td><td></td><td></td><td></td></tr>
<tr><td>Aug</td><td>22</td><td>1 Canister Powder 88¢ ...</td><td>..</td><td>88</td></tr>
<tr><td>Sept</td><td>22</td><td>Boots 400¢ Socks 50¢ alum 13¢</td><td>4</td><td>63</td></tr>
<tr><td>"</td><td>"</td><td>Suspenders 125¢ Nails 13¢ pepper 19¢</td><td>1</td><td>56</td></tr>
<tr><td>"</td><td>"</td><td>2 Shoes 300¢ Buttons 25¢ .. ..</td><td>3</td><td>25</td></tr>
<tr><td>Oct</td><td>7</td><td>cot. Whf 37½¢ 5lb coffee 100¢ -</td><td>1</td><td>38</td></tr>
<tr><td>"</td><td>14</td><td>spelling book 19¢</td><td>..</td><td>19</td></tr>
<tr><td>Nov</td><td>1</td><td>combs 50¢ Cabinet 450¢ teas 37½¢ ...</td><td>5</td><td>38</td></tr>
<tr><td>"</td><td>"</td><td>Spoons 25¢ Plates 75¢ torque 100¢ why 75¢</td><td>2</td><td>75</td></tr>
<tr><td>1837</td><td>5</td><td>Cash 300¢ Deer 14lb Shoes 100¢ Boots 350¢ 7.60</td><td>8</td><td>27.52</td></tr>
<tr><td>Jany</td><td>8</td><td>Coffee 200¢ Sugar 100¢ Whks 75¢</td><td>3</td><td>75</td></tr>
<tr><td>"</td><td>17</td><td>Coffee 100¢ Whk 30¢ Knife 63¢</td><td>1</td><td>94</td></tr>
<tr><td>"</td><td>21</td><td>Why 12¢ auger 38¢ hammer 75¢ Needles 19¢</td><td>1</td><td>44</td></tr>
<tr><td>"</td><td>"</td><td>twist 13¢ Feb 2nd Coffee 1.00¢</td><td>1.12</td><td>8.25</td></tr>
<tr><td></td><td></td><td></td><td>$35.77</td><td></td></tr>
<tr><td>1838</td><td></td><td></td><td></td><td></td></tr>
<tr><td>Apl</td><td>1</td><td>To pa saw nw 19 Ballance on Bridle 50lb</td><td>1.68</td><td></td></tr>
<tr><td>March</td><td>19</td><td>Cuts filling pens</td><td>25</td><td></td></tr>
<tr><td></td><td></td><td></td><td>93</td><td></td></tr>
</table>

Critendon Forguerean   Dr

1836 $ cts

Sept 28 1 pr Shoes 1.70, Oct 22 Brandy & quality 2.59   2 2 9 2.25

Nov 20 Aloes 12 1/2, Why 38, Crackers 13, Shoes 18   2   13

Jan 4   Salt 4.56, Why 25, Cash 50   5   31

1837
Jany 4 Salt 5.17   5   17   12.61

Feb 5   Sheeting 5.44, Brandy 18, Nickel 2.59   6   32   6.32

                                              18.93

1837 $ 63

March 19 x ten pans 1.50 x Chocolate 50   2   00

Peter Gillis

156   Peter Gillis   Dr
1836
Sept 23 a pr fine Shoes 1.75 1pt Brandy 25   2 00
Deer 31 Casinett 10.13 Casinett 6.25   16 38
" 1837 twist 12/9   13 $985
Jany 28 Draper 300 --   --   --   3 06
                                                  2 151
1839
april 4 shoe nippers hammer & tacks   2 85

Isaac Gray   Dr

1836 $ 6

Aug 29   1 gallon Why 75¢ 1. Augg 38¢ ― ― ―   1 13
Sept 19   Salt 1.10¢ Shoes 150¢ 2 60
  "   24   Brandy 13¢ 25th Socks 50¢ Why 13¢   .. 75
  "   28   Why 75¢ Oct 1st Why 25¢ 1 00
oct   7   8 yds casinet 1.10.0¢ & Brandy 13¢   10 08
  "   8   Brandy 13¢ 14th 2 Knails 19¢ 1 gall Why 100¢   2 13
  ..   14   curry comb 19¢ paid John Boon $10 ..   10 19
  "   16   Why 12¢ 17th nails 50¢ Why 12¢ 18th cap 100¢ 6 75
  "   23   Why 12¢ 24th Why 25¢   38
  "   25   Coffee 100¢ Why 75¢ turpentine 12¢ Why 2 00
  "   "   Wine 13¢ wine 12¢ 30th Why 50¢   75
Nov 5   Why 75¢ Lot teas 100¢ ― ― ― ―   1 75
  "   10   Why 12¢ 20th pd John Boon 250¢   2 68
Dec   1   Coffee 1.00¢ 2d Why 88¢ Sugar 100¢   2 88
  "   7   Why 75¢ 13th padding 50¢ Needles 13¢   1 38
  "   16   Why 13¢ 18th Knife 12 5¢   1 38
  "   25   Stew 25¢ Why 13¢ 26th Stew 25¢   63
1837
Jany 4   Why 75¢ Wine 25¢ Rice 13¢ 6th Stew 25¢   1 38
  "   7   Cap 100¢ Stew 25¢ 8th Why 92¢ Stew 13¢   1 51 $5 1
Jany 9   Wine 25¢ Stew 13¢ 14th Why 13¢   51
  "   17   Stew 13¢ Why 25¢ 20th Knife 12 5¢   1 63
  "   20   Duck 25¢ Why 13¢ 21st flask 13¢   .. 51
  "   25   Ink Stand 25¢ Wine 13¢ Brandy 13¢   .. 51
  "   27   Nails 50¢ " ― ― " ― ― "   .. 50
Feb   11   flask Why 25 ¢ Brandy 13¢ " ― ― "   .. 38
  "   20   Why 25¢ 36th Why 25¢ " ― ― "   .. 50
  "   28   1 qrm Bottle Why 50¢   .. 50
March 4   nails 62¢ Why 13¢   75   5 0
                                                        5 6 0

58   Isaac Gray   Dr

1847 $ cts

april 20 shoes 2.69 tumblers 50 why 19   2 69
"   "   plate 37½ coffee 1.50   1 38
          pd why 25   25
may 22   why 13 20 may why 25 why 12   . 50
     30   1 Bridle 2.50 june 5 why 38 why 12 88
June 13   9 lbs sugar - 1.00   1 00
may 5   Cash Loand 2.00   2 00
June 13   Plank & whis   25
     24   why 13 why 12 june 25 board 31   57
     26   whis 13 27 whis 25 whis 13   50
     20   whis 13 whis 25 whis 12   50
July 1   Shoes 1.63 chip hat 75 whis 12   2 50
     1   do 38 & Tacks 3 Shoes 3.50   3 88
          whis 13 they July Egg 3 why 11   25
     7   whis 1st the 8 july salt 75 whis 13 62
     11   whis 38 whis 37   75
     18   shaving soap 6 whis 13   19
     20   1 lb candles 50 1 gallon whis 75 1 15
     11   whis 13 the 2 July whis 25   38
august 1 whis 25 the 4 of augus 13 all 25   50
     4   why 38 tea arone 37   75
     12   why 13 Boots 4.25 Brush 25   4 63
     13   why 25 tin tumblers 38   63
     11   Sugar 1.68 A.S.   1 68
     29   why 13 why 12   25
sept 12   why 75 candle moulds 75 why 11   1 62
     13   whis 25   25
     16   1 Glass whis 13   13
                                            29 78
     12   why why 50 to cash loand 4.00   4 00
                                           37 40
See Page 73   Cr 13   37 38
                                          $ 7 04
                                           57 04

73　　　ISAAC Gray　Dr　$　c

1837
Dec 17　Jn 1 ltt Rasins 17c 1oz 2 Glass Whis 25c　　　42
　　24　" 1/2 pt whis 13 Jan 9th 19th whis 25 = 3 Dn 13　$　56
　　28　" Brot amount from Page 38　　　37　04
1838　　　Hitchcock B C keeping　　$ c　43
Jan 22　" 1 Curel McComb 19. Feb 3 = Dist 12.no　12.19　434 5
Feb 9　" To 3 Drms 1 Gall cohes 119c 11 1 penknif 78　1.94
　" 11　" Steer c 50 17th 1 Gallon Whis 100. 3 Gelling　4.50
Mch　" 6 = Jug 38 1 Glass 5c Jr 2 Glass Whis 25　1 13
　　9　" Dist with Minscott ♉ 8.29. 2 Glass Whis 25　8.54
　13　" Sundries 99.50 = 25 = Ju 38 = 17 Sund 169 =　3.23
Apr 6　" Sund 69 = 7 = Sund 38　1.07
　7　one palm Leaf Hatt　50
　12　1 lb rasins 38. May 3 1 plate Augso　86

　　　　　　　　3458

　　　　　　　　75.03
　　　　　　　　11 25

　　　　　　Cr　66 78
　　　　　　　　5.50

　　　　　　　　61. 28
　　　　　　　　43 50

　　　　　　　　17 78
　　　　　　　　17.78

A. W. Harlan

108   Aaron W. Harlon   Dr

1835

Aug 28   1 Shaving Box & Soap 31 1 qt Why 25₵   6
    "   & dirk Knife 63₵ 1 canister powder 87₵   1 56
Sept 12   1 pr Socks 50₵ 1 Sack 25₵ 1 yd doms 12½   " 88
    "   4 H Nails 100₵ 2 qts Why 50₵   "   2 50
    26   1 stock 1.25₵ Nov 10 ½ drawers 1.25₵   2 50
Nov 10   Knife 1.75₵ 16th Brandy 25₵   2 00
    22   Drawers 1.25₵ calico 75₵   2 00
    23   Why 75₵ ....   "   75.11.69
Decr 2   Boots 450 & 7th Nails 100₵ Stand 25₵   5 75
    18   flask & Why 25 & 20th Wine 12₵ Collar 150₵ 1 88
    22   Chisell 30 & 24th firkin 12½₵   63
    26   Casimere 9.76₵ Socks 50₵ Drill 12₵ Why 13₵ 10 50
    "1836 Twist & Silk 25 27th Bbl 75₵ Comb 37½₵ 1 38 $20.14
Sept 29 Pepper & Bag 19 & Best coarse Shoes 175₵   1 94
March 4 Sundry articles   9 20
    18   Vest Patton 175₵ Socks 100₵   "   2 75
    19   Soap 12½₵ Needles 18½₵   31 14.20
                                          34.34

8
1856   William Jorden   Dr

June 5 from small ledger page 19   39 99
" 10 1 gall milk pan 95¢ coffee mill 80¢ 1 75
" " 10¢ cot yarn 375¢ & 3. indigo 80¢ mader 17¢ 4 68
" " Broom 25¢ hoe 75¢ file 30¢ sheep bells 1 75
" " dish 37¢ 1 do 19¢ & tobacco 25¢ 81
" 27 beef 50¢ Bobinet 25¢ 75
July 23 1 pr fine shoes 175¢ 9 tb 119 salt 129 turpentine 2 37
aug 7 1 tobacco 25¢ 25 52 93

Aug 21 1/4 t Cream tarter 38¢ 38
oct 15 1 pr shoes 40¢ & griddle 75¢ 5 lb coffee 100¢ 4 25
" " linen bucket 75¢ curtain calico 600¢ 6 75
" " sheeting 137¢ nails 100¢ claw hamr 75¢ 3 63
Nov 11 tobacco 25¢ Crackers 12½¢ 38
Dec 12 Saw 150¢ Comb 31¢ 1 81 1720
Jany 20 Plaid 352¢ Diaper 300¢ Knives forks 250¢ 9 02
" " Socks 50¢ teas 100¢ Blankets 1200 13 50
" " Sheeting 540¢ Combs 50¢ Coffee 200¢ 7 90 30 49
$47 69

Daniel. Mc Mullen   Dr

1856
Sept 7   3 yds flannel 3½ & 14 cotton 50¢   1 63
   "   1 Lamp ...... 10.00 .... 30 00
          flannel 3d 1 pr drawers &3   81
 d 14   1 lb Tobacco 30¢ taxes &5 1 pr gloves 38¢   1 33
          5 yd linsey 1.55 shoes 1.85 socks 20¢ .. 3 32
          7 yd cloth 5.25 3 gloves 50¢   5 75
          by cash Sent to J. Sailor 100.00
             Sundry articles   8 24
          by cash   400.00
April 12 by Cash   3300
                                                763.58
May 23   by cash .... "   77 56
august 4th by cash   338 31
                                               1179 45
Oct 24th   & Cash   387 21
                                               1560 66
April 6th to Cash Collected   41 31

          Settled April 28th 1858

1858
Jan 21 To Sundries 5.62 Feb 3 Cash 30.00   35.62

64   William Phelps   Dr

		$	C
1836			
august 21	To sundries $ 1.80 . . .	1	80
Sept 9	1 British oil 8¢ p d. Samuel Beaver	1	08
25	Cash 10.50 ¢ 28 d. flannel 5.25¢ Glove 100¢	16	75
oct 11	Boots 2.80¢ salaratus 100¢ flasks 60.08¢	4	00
,, 22	Suspenders 75¢ mens annt ment 25¢	1	00
,, 26	domestic 123¢ thread buttons 25¢ - -	1	48
,, 28	Laudanum 25¢ shirt Wh¢ 37/¢ .	..	63
Nov. 6	Casomere 2.00¢ Cambric 25¢	2	25
,, ,,	Buckram 25¢ twist & silk 37/¢ buttons 13¢	..	75
,, ,,	Sheeting 21¢	21	$29.95
Feb 9	~~James 44¢~~ Gloves 80¢¢ Casinett 2.34¢3	3	13
1837			
Sept 22	pills 25¢ c. oil 50¢ dippher 19¢	..	81
....	candles 25¢	..	25
..	1 ps avr. Hams	1	75
	2 viles Cordial	..	50
	12 D of Candles	..	25
		3	05

Glossary:

&c.	etcetera or etc.
abated	reduced to normal
about home	that is "at home" or on the farm
akimbo	with hands on the hips and elbows turned outward.
alcade	(in Spain and Spanish America) the mayor or chief magistrate in a town.
alloy	an alloy is commonly a substance added to improve a character of metal. In this archaic usage, it means whisky to provide stamina.
animus	hostility or ill feeling
Appanoose	Meskwaki chief who lived in Iowa; he was son of Taimah (Chief Tama)
ascertained	find (something) out for certain; make sure of.
Baptist Hard Shells	Primitive Baptist Church that was against the missionary spirit, Sunday School, preacher salary, theology schools, temperance societies, etc.
bedizened	dress up or decorate gaudily.
biles	slang or misspelling for boils
billet	a place, usually a civilian's house or other nonmilitary facility, where soldiers are lodged temporarily.
BlackHawk War	Blackhawk war 1832, US Military attacked Blackhawk's tribe when they tired to re-settle on natïve lands where they found their native burial grounds plowed and bones exposed by the settlers.

i

brandished	wave or flourish (something, especially a weapon) as a threat or in anger or excitement
catamount	cat of the mountain - cougar
Che-che-pe-qua	Indian name for Bill Phelps
cholera	an acute diarrhea disease that can kill within hours if untreated.
cite	misspelling of site or location
commonwealth	a political community founded for the common good.
conciliate	stop (someone) from being angry or discontented; placate; pacify
concocting	create or devise
Coon River	Raccoon River in Des Moines
corpulent	fat or overweight
crupper	a strap buckled to the back of a saddle and looped under the horse's tail to prevent the saddle or harness from slipping forward
details	a small detachment of troops or police officers given a special duty.
Devil	primary opponent of God, the tempter
discreet	careful and circumspect in one's speech or actions, especially in order to avoid causing offense or to gain an advantage.
dissipated	overindulging in sensual pleasures, whiskey & women
dissipation	a descent into drunkenness and sexual dissipation
divulged	make known (private or sensitive information)
doggery	US slang. A disreputable drinking establishment
dram	a dram is equivalent to about ½ Cup (.469 Cup)
dyspeptic	having indigestion or consequent irritability or depression

eatables	slang for food
ebullition	a sudden outburst of emotion or violence
Elenois	misspelling or slang for Illinois
empanneled	selected for jury duty
encomiums	a speech or piece of writing that praises someone or something highly
ensconced	establish or settle (someone) in a comfortable, safe, or secret place
exultation	rejoicing or Triumphant elation
exulting	show or feel elation or jubilation, especially as the result of a success
facetious	treating serious issues with deliberately inappropriate humor; flippant.
fee simple	a permanent and absolute tenure of an estate in land with freedom to dispose of it at will (the main type of land ownership today.)
flatboat	usually a one way vehicle to haul goods downriver. Flat bottom up to 20' wide and up to 100' long.
Fort Pike	Fort Pike was constructed at St. Francisville, MO in 1832.
freshet	a freshet is the spring thaw of the streams and river. Quite often they result in an ice jam and flood the river up-river. One of the most deadly situations for the early settlers.
frolicking	play and move about cheerfully, excitedly, or energetically
fuddled	confused or stupefied, especially as a result of drinking alcohol
gerrymandering	manipulating voting districts to benefit one party
grog shop	a low class barroom
hallooed	cry or shout "halloo" to attract attention
harem	the wives of a polygamous man

harr	slang or misspelling for hair
hierogriphical	symbols almost impossible to understand
hollow	yell loudly to be found (holler)
imbroglio	an extremely confused, complicated, or embarrassing situation
Independent	the current town of Selma, also called Stumptown
Indian lodge	the house of the Midwest Indian's made of sticks and bark.
Indian trader	someone who trades goods with the Indians, usually for a fur company.
indignant	feeling or showing anger or annoyance at what is perceived as unfair treatment.
infidel	a person who does not believe in a religion or God.
Ingersoll, Bob	a famous agnostic who constantly ridiculed religion.
inimitable	so good or unusual as to be impossible to copy; unique.
interpreter	translator for military with Indians
isthmus	a narrow strip of land with sea on either side, forming a link between two larger areas of land; in this case Panama, about 50 miles overland. (No canal existed until 1914
ivory	slang for teeth
jam of fence	the interior corner of intersection or crossing of a log fence
junketing	taking an excursion for pleasure.
jury trial	trial by jury, a panel of peers.
keel boat	a shallow narrow or cigar shaped cargo boat designed to haul goods up river by pole.

latch string	a string that is attached to the door latch. Can be placed on the outside so the door can be opened from the outside, or pulled inside to lock the door to outside visitors.
laurels	wreath or crown and worn on the head as an emblem of victory or mark of honor in classical times
lead	to be in charge or command of "his life"
leggings	buckskin or wool blanket leg coverings
legion	meaning many, as the group of demons Jesus drove out of a man, 3000 men in a Roman army
lind	wood from a linden or basswood tree
lionized	give a lot of public attention and approval to (someone); treat as a celebrity
liquor	a drink of any alcoholic beverage, usually whisky in the pioneer days.
lisp	a speech defect in which s is pronounced like th in "thick" and z is pronounced like th in "this"
lob-lolly	a thick gruel; mire, or mud hole
loth	reluctant; unwilling.
ludicrous	so foolish, unreasonable, or out of place as to be amusing; ridiculous
manifested	display or show (a quality or feeling) by one's acts or appearance; demonstrate
martial law	military government involving the suspension of ordinary law.
measles	highly contagious disease that caused between 3-4 million deaths before immunization in the US. By 2016, the America's claim it has been eliminated here.
Methodist Circuit Rider	an early form of Methodist preacher who traveled thought the US on horse back and preached in open fields to the

settlers.

Missouri War	a short squirmish between Iowa and Missouri over the boundary and taxes of that area concerned. It came very close to being an all out war. The US
mollified	appease the anger or anxiety of (someone)
Morpheus	the Greek God of Dreams
old sledge	card game similar to pitch without bidding – High, Low, Jack, Game also called Seven-up
orchard	in settling the Northwest Territory, settlers were required to plat 50 apple trees and 20 peach trees to prove their settlement permanent and keep their land grant.
ordance	a branch of the armed forces dealing with the supply and storage of weapons, ammunition, and related equipment.
overweening	showing excessive confidence or pride.
owing	due to, or was caused by
peevler creek	a creek or small stream in Elm Bottom
per diem	per day in Latin.
perogatives	a right or privilege exclusive to a particular individual or class
pirouke	or pea rogue (French for hollowed out log canoe)
ploughed	spelling for plowed, outside the US and Canada; same with plough vs. plow
polygamist	a person who has more than one wife or husband at the same time.
prairie chickens	once a very abundant bird on the prairie is now primarily limited to prairie areas in Kansas, Nebraska and South Dakota

Presbyterian Church	the Presbyterian Church was primarily a Lutheran Reformation of Scottish settlers governed by an assembly of elders. in the US. Most areas of Scottish immigration were Presbyterian in faith.
present he distribute	success with the squaws he had
prostrated	reduced (someone) to extreme physical weakness
punchon	split log or roughly formed lumber for a floor in settler cabins.
queensware crate	queensware (inexpensive cream china from England) was shipped from England to America, up the Mississippi in large wooden crates
rendezvoused	to meet or come together at an agreed time and place.
riffle	a rocky or shallow part of a stream or river with rough water
Santa Fe bears	bears from Santa Fe, NM
scalp lock	a long lock of hair left on a shaved head, especially as worn by a North American Indian as a challenge to enemies.
scalping knife	a knife similar to a butcher knife used by the Native Americans to scalp their victims. Originally was a stone knife before the English trade.
seven up	card game similar to pitch without bidding – High, Low, Jack, Game also called Old Sledge
she-se-pac	sugar (maple sugar)
Skine--way	Indian for young man or boy
spree	a spell or sustained period of unrestrained activity of a particular kind.
spurious	not being what it purports to be; false or fake.
Squawl	alternave spelling of squall - cry noisily and continuously.
Stiff	slang -racehorse or someone sure to loose

stroke	snake attempt to bite or strike
suffrance	alt spelling of sufferance enduring of hardship, affliction, etc.; allowance of wrong doing
Sugar Creek	a creek or small stream that runs from near Mt Hamill, IA to extreme SE Iowa on Des Moines River.
Sullivan Line	The Iowa/Missouri line today (was the border between Indian Territory and Missouri when surveyed)
superfluous	unnecessary, especially through being more than enough.
tackies	Marsh Tacky rare breed of South Carolina horse descended from Spanish colonial horses
tantrum	an uncontrolled outburst of anger and frustration, typically in a young child.
tanyard	an area of a tannery set aside for the operation of tanning vats
tare	on a spree, drinking, or winning
telephone	hard to believe, but the telephone was invented in 1876, Bell Telephone Company was founded 7/9/1877, by 2/17/1878 phone exchanges existed in Connecticut and San Francisco.
tempter	Devil - a person or thing that tempts
tit-bit	a small piece of tasty food - nickname of Blackhawk's youngest wife
tomahawk	a stone axe developed by the Native American Indians, later was made of metal and became one of the popular trade goods in the fur trade.
topographer	a person who describes the surface features of a place or region
transmognified	transform, especially in a surprising or magical manner.
traps	personal belongings; baggage.

tribulation	a state of great trouble or suffering.
T'y	abbreviation for Territory
US Rangers	military unit of mounted infantry formed for war of 1812, disbanded in 1815. Reformed in 1832 for Black Hawk War, became 1st Dragon Regiment in 1833.
usfruct	the right to enjoy the use and advantages of another's property short of the destruction or waste of its substance.
vallet de chambre	a court appointment introduced in the late Middle Ages, common from the 14th century onwards a manservant who acts as a personal attendant to his employer.
vedettes	a mounted sentry positioned beyond an army's outposts to observe the movements of the enemy
vermillion	a brilliant red or scarlet pigment originally made from the powdered mineral cinnabar
virginian	a settler from Virginia
Wabash Prairie	Prairie near Montrose, IA
wammus	warm linen work jacket resembling a Cardigan
Washinngton City	Washington DC
welkin ring	loud shout rejoicing or celebrating
whiskey	Irish spelling of Scottish Whisky, also the spelling for American whiskey.
wooden hourse	a torture device similar to a saw horse where the person is seated straddle of the device for a certain amount of time, sometimes with weights tied to the legs.
wrung	past tense of wring to squeeze or twist especially so as to make dry or to extract moisture or liquid – to get everything

yellow fever	a deadly viral disease caused by mosquito bites. Can be deadly since no cure is known. Can cause liver damage, internal bleeding, kidney damage etc. Was considered one of the most dangerous diseases in the 18th and 19th centuries. Vaccination is required if traveling in many countries of the world.
yellow ochre	ochre, is a natural earth pigment containing hydrated iron oxide, which ranges in color from yellow to deep orange or brown

INDEX:

Notes:

www.ingramcontent.com/pod-product-compliance
Lightning Source LLC
Chambersburg PA
CBHW060050100426
42742CB00014B/2760